Collins

T0337234

Year 2
Maths & English
Targeted Study
& Practice Book

Jon Goulding and Brad Thompson

How to use this book

This Maths and English Study and Practice book contains everything children need for the school year in one book.

A **study page** and a **practice page** for each topic.

'Remember' boxes highlight key points

Tips give ideas on how to remember key information.

Key words highlighted on each Study page with definitions in the glossary.

Questions split into three levels of difficulty – **Challenge 1**, **Challenge 2** and **Challenge 3** – to help progression.

Total marks boxes for recording progress and **'How am I doing'** checks for self-evaluation.

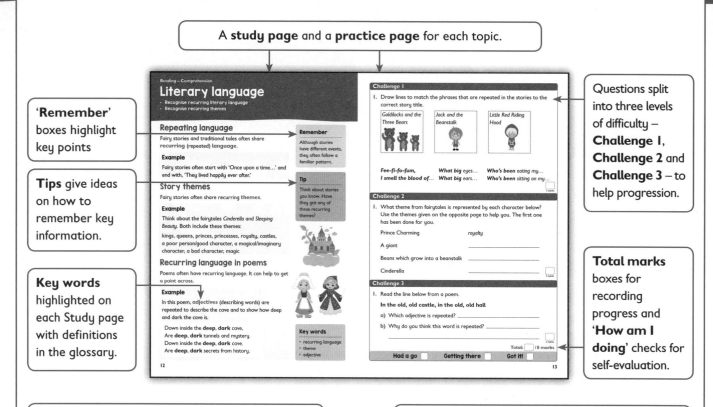

Four **Progress tests** included throughout the book for ongoing assessment and monitoring progress.

Mixed questions for maths and English test topics from throughout the book.

Problem-solving questions identified with a clear symbol.

Answers provided for all the questions.

Contents

Sounds and words

- Recognise alternative sounds for letters

Same letter, different sound

Sometimes, the same letter (**grapheme**) can make a different sound (**phoneme**) in different words.

Example

g – The **g**entle **g**iant has some **g**old.

If the **g** comes before a, o or u, it has a **g** sound, e.g. **g**old, **g**ap.

If the **g** comes before e, i or y, it usually has a **j** sound, e.g. **g**entle, **g**iant. (Exceptions are **g**et and **g**i**gg**le.)

j – It took an a**ge** to **j**og round the e**dge** of the lake.

A **j** sound at the beginning of a word before a, o or u is spelt with a **j**, e.g. **j**og, **j**oin.

A **j** sound at the end of a word is not spelt with a **j**:
- After a short vowel sound, the letters **-dge** are used, e.g. e**dge**, fu**dge**.
- After all other sounds, the letters **-ge** are used, e.g. a**ge**, pa**ge**.

c – The **c**at lives in the shopping **c**entre in the **c**ity.

If the **c** comes before e, i or y it has the sound represented by the **s** in **s**nake, e.g. **c**entre, **c**ity, i**c**y.

If the **c** comes before a, o, u or l, it has the sound represented by the **k** in **k**ing, e.g. **c**at, **c**ling, **c**urd.

Two other sounds you need to be able to recognise are:
- the **r** sound represented by the **r** in run, written as **wr**, e.g. **wr**ite, **wr**ap. $\longleftarrow$ [w is a **silent letter** in these words]
- the **n** sound represented by the **n** in nip, written as **kn** and **gn**, e.g. **kn**ow, **kn**ock, **gn**at, **gn**aw. $\longleftarrow$ [**k** and **g** are silent letters in these words]

> **Tip**
>
> Short vowel sounds are: 'a' as in 'cat', 'e' as in 'bed', 'i' as in 'tin', 'o' as in 'hot' and 'u' as in 'up'.

> **Remember**
>
> If you are unsure about a word, read the whole sentence as this might give you a clue.

> **Key words**
>
> - graphemes
> - phonemes
> - silent letters

Challenge 1

1. Read the words. Circle each word that has a **j** sound, as in **j**am.

gold   giant   gent

gap   gem   gull

great

3 marks

Challenge 2

1. Write the words below in the correct boxes.

cat   cliff   city   race   cold   rice   fancy   claw

c making a **k** sound

c making a **s** sound

8 marks

Challenge 3

1. Read the words and draw lines to match them to the correct sentence.

know   Seb _____ a letter.

wrong   I hurt my _____ .

knee   We went the _____ way.

wrote   Do you _____ the answer?

4 marks

Total: _____ / 15 marks

Had a go		Getting there		Got it!	

Words and syllables

- Blend sounds in longer words
- Read words with two or more syllables

Syllables

Each 'beat' in a word is known as a **syllable**.

Example

Short words have just one beat or syllable:

edge

jar

badge

hat

Many words have two syllables:

magic (mag/ic)   writer (wri/ter)   gentle (gen/tle)

Each syllable has its own **vowel** sound:

mum

cam/el

Breaking words into syllables can be helpful when trying to read and write them.

Try clapping the syllables for each word below as you read it aloud:

app/le   cap/it/al   in/cred/ib/le

two syllables   three syllables   four syllables

Look at these words that have two or more syllables. See how the final syllable in each word sounds similar even though some are written differently.

tab/le   suit/ab/le   tins/el   un/rav/el
ped/al   an/im/al   penc/il   foss/il

Challenge 1

1. Read each word below and write how many syllables it has.

squirrel   **quantity**   **middle**   **written**   **energy**

____ syllables   ____ syllables   ____ syllables   ____ syllables   ____ syllables

5 marks

Challenge 2

1. Draw lines to match each clue to the correct word. Check your answer by counting the syllables.

Another word for a creature (3 syllables)   giraffe

A very, very big person (2 syllables)   hospital

An animal with a long neck (2 syllables)   bottle

Something a drink might be in (2 syllables)   animal

You might go here if you are ill (3 syllables)   giant

5 marks

Challenge 3

1. Read the text below. Underline every word that has two or more syllables.

On the floor was a strange animal. It looked a bit like a rabbit. It was

wrapping itself up carefully in a blanket. Next to it was a table.

In the middle of that was a pencil and a metal water bottle with a

large capital letter written on the side.

15 marks

Total: ____ / 25 marks

Had a go ☐   Getting there ☐   Got it! ☐

Word endings

- Know that the spelling of some words changes before adding a suffix
- Read words ending in -s, -es, -ed, -er, -est and -ing where the root word has been changed

Adding -s and -es

Words can be changed by adding an ending, known as a **suffix**. Adding **-s** or **-es** to a **root word** changes it from **singular** (one) to **plural** (more than one).

Example

The suffix **-es** is added to words ending in **-s**, **-x**, **-h** and **-y** to make them plural.

class ⇨ class**es**   fox ⇨ fox**es**
church ⇨ church**es**   baby ⇨ bab**ies**

For words ending in **y**, the **y** is changed to **i** before adding **-es**, e.g. sk**y** ⇨ sk**ies**. ◄

> If there is a vowel before 'y', just **-s** is added, e.g. tra**y** ⇨ tra**ys**.

Tip

Use picture clues to help you see if there is more than one of something.

Remember

A root word is a basic word without letters added to the start or end. When reading a word with a suffix, it may help to work out the root word first.

Adding -ed, -er, -est and -ing to words ending in y

If a word ends in **-y** with any letter other than a **vowel** before it, the **-y** is replaced with an **i** before the suffix is added.

copy ⇨ cop**ied**   cry ⇨ cr**ied**   happy ⇨ happ**iest**
reply ⇨ repl**ied**   silly ⇨ sill**iest**   happy ⇨ happ**ier** ◄

> When reading these words, the **i** makes the same sound as the **y** in the root word.

But the **y** is not changed to **i** before adding **-ing**.

copy ⇨ copy**ing**   cry ⇨ cry**ing**   reply ⇨ reply**ing**

When adding the suffixes **-ment**, **-ness**, **-ful**, **-less** and **-ly**, there is no change to the last letter of the root word:

settle**ment**   sad**ness**   care**ful**   use**less**   slow**ly**

But words such as happy, silly and merry have the **y** replaced with **i** before adding the suffix:

happiness   silliness   merriment

Key words

- suffix
- root word
- singular
- plural
- vowel

Challenge 1

1. Join each related word from each column. The first one has been done for you.

happy	carrying	flying
copy	replied	happiest
reply	flies	copier
carry	happier	carried
fly	copied	replying

4 marks

Challenge 2

1. Write the root word for the underlined word in each sentence.

a) The teacher was <u>grumpier</u> than usual. _____

b) Ross was <u>careless</u> when he bumped his head. _____

c) It looks like the weather is <u>changing</u>. _____

d) The rain did not stop their <u>enjoyment</u>. _____

4 marks

Challenge 3

1. Complete the passage below. Use the root words below and add the correct endings.

happy   cry   care   baby   play

The nursery was busy but the **b**_____ were not **c**_____.

The staff were being **c**_____ not to wake them. Some of

the toddlers were **h**_____ than others but they were all

p_____ .

5 marks

Total: [ ] / 13 marks

Had a go [ ]	Getting there [ ]	Got it! [ ]

9

Common exception words

- Read common exception words
- Be aware of unusual spellings of sounds in these words

Tricky words

Common exception words can be tricky because the sounds in the words do not follow normal spelling rules.

Example

mind	find	blind	behind
cold	hold	told	gold

> These words do not end in **e** so it would be easy to think that the vowels **i** and **o** would be the short sounds represented in t**i**n and m**o**p.

Other examples include:

- **ea** would normally sound like it does in **ea**t, **ea**ch, b**ea**t, but:
  - in these words it makes the long **a** sound as in l**a**te:
    gr**ea**t   st**ea**k   br**ea**k
  - in these words it makes the short **e** sound as in b**e**d:
    h**ea**d   br**ea**d   r**ea**d
- In the words **s**ugar and **s**ure, the letter **s** makes a **sh** sound.
- In the words **coul**d, **woul**d and sh**oul**d, the letters **oul** make the sound represented by **u** in c**u**p.
- In the word b**u**sy, the letter **u** makes the sound represented by **i** in t**i**n.
- In the word p**eo**ple, the letters **eo** make the sound represented by **ee** in p**ee**p.

Words to learn

Try to learn the exception words on this page:

> mind, find, blind, behind, cold, hold, told, gold, great, steak, break, head, bread, read, sugar, sure, would, could, should, busy, people.

Remember

Read the whole sentence to help you work out tricky words.

Tip

Keep a look out for exception words. Write them down and practise saying and spelling them.

Key word

- common exception word

Challenge 1

1. The words on the left have been spelt incorrectly. Draw lines to match each one to its correct spelling on the right.

shud   sugar

shugar   should

shure   sure

Challenge 2

1. Write each tricky word in the correct sentence.

   would   **should**   **could**

   a) This _____ be a great day.

   b) I _____ like a cake please.

   c) You _____ know better.

Challenge 3

1. a) Read the text. Make sure you can clearly read aloud the underlined exception words.

   > It was a <u>beautiful</u> day. <u>Wild</u> flowers grew by the edge of the <u>water</u>. <u>Most</u> <u>people</u> <u>could</u> not see this <u>great</u> place. <u>Even</u> in the winter, Sam <u>would</u> <u>climb</u> the hill <u>every</u> day to look at the sight.

   b) Practise writing the underlined exception words from the text above.

   _____

   _____

   _____

   _____

Total: ☐ / 17 marks

Had a go ☐   **Getting there** ☐   **Got it!** ☐

Literary language

- Recognise recurring literary language
- Recognise recurring themes

Repeating language

Fairy stories and traditional tales often share **recurring** (repeated) **language**.

Example

Fairy stories often start with 'Once upon a time…' and end with, 'They lived happily ever after.'

Story themes

Fairy stories often share recurring **themes**.

Example

Think about the fairytales *Cinderella* and *Sleeping Beauty*. Both include these themes:

kings, queens, princes, princesses, royalty, castles, a poor person/good character, a magical/imaginary character, a bad character, magic

Recurring language in poems

Poems often have recurring language. It can help to get a point across.

Example

In this poem, **adjectives** (describing words) are repeated to describe the cave and to show how deep and dark the cave is.

> Down inside the **deep**, **dark** cave,
> Are **deep**, **dark** tunnels and mystery.
> Down inside the **deep**, **dark** cave.
> Are **deep**, **dark** secrets from history.

Remember

Although stories have different events, they often follow a familiar pattern.

Tip

Think about stories you know. Have they got any of these recurring themes?

Key words

- recurring language
- theme
- adjective

Challenge 1

1. Draw lines to match the phrases that are repeated in the stories to the correct story title.

Goldilocks and the Three Bears	*Jack and the Beanstalk*	*Little Red Riding Hood*

Fee-fi-fo-fum,
I smell the blood of...

What big eyes…
What big ears…

Who's been eating my…
Who's been sitting on my…

3 marks

Challenge 2

1. What theme from fairytales is represented by each character below? Use the themes given on the opposite page to help you. The first one has been done for you.

Prince Charming   *royalty*

A giant   _____

Beans which grow into a beanstalk   _____

Cinderella   _____

3 marks

Challenge 3

1. Read the line below from a poem.

In the old, old castle, in the old, old hall

a) Which adjective is repeated? _____

b) Why do you think this word is repeated? _____

_____

2 marks

Total: ☐ /8 marks

| Had a go ☐ | Getting there ☐ | Got it! ☐ |

13

Events in stories

- Understand how events in a story are related

Story parts

A **fiction** story is a made-up story with characters and events that make it interesting, exciting and enjoyable to read. The events are related to each other in a **sequence**. One event must happen before the next one can.

Tip

Think about how the events are related to each other in other stories you know.

Example

Jack and the Beanstalk

Beginning

Once upon a time, Jack sold his cow for magic beans.

This part has to happen before the magic beans are thrown and a beanstalk grows.

Middle

Jack climbs the beanstalk. At the top he sees a castle and a giant.

This has to happen before Jack gets chased by the giant.

End

Jack climbs down the beanstalk. His mother cuts it down.

Jack makes his escape and the beanstalk is chopped down. Jack is safe.

Remember

Most good stories have a beginning, a middle and an end.

New words and meanings

You might come across some new words when you are reading a story. Sometimes you need to work out their meaning to help your understanding.

Example

*Jack **cautiously** approached the castle.*
What does cautiously mean? You know that Jack was being careful when he approached, so 'cautiously' must be another word for 'careful'.

Key words

- fiction
- sequence

Challenge 1

1. Number the events **1**, **2**, **3** and **4** to put the events in the correct order.

Jack climbed the beanstalk.	A beanstalk grew in the garden.	Jack sold his cow and got magic beans.	Jack saw the giant at the top.
☐	☐	☐	☐

4 marks

Challenge 2

1. Read the text and then answer the questions.

Adventure beneath the sea

The submarine dived under the waves. There were fish of all colours, shapes and sizes. There was a similar variety of shells too. The children sat and stared with their eyes and mouths open wide. This was already a great adventure. They loved the ocean.

a) Which word shows that there were lots of different shells? _____

b) Circle the word that describes how the children were feeling.

amazed   **scared**   **bored**

c) What is another word for ocean? _____

3 marks

Challenge 3

1. Write a word with a similar meaning to each underlined word.

a) Goldilocks <u>reclined</u> in the chair. _____

b) Jack <u>clambered</u> up the beanstalk. _____

c) Cinderella <u>hastily</u> ran home. _____

3 marks

Total: ☐ / 10 marks

Had a go ☐	**Getting there** ☐	**Got it!** ☐

Poetry

- Discuss and interpret words and phrases in poems

What is a poem?

Poems tell stories, share ideas and describe objects and feelings. Words in poems often **rhyme**.

The words used for description in a poem help paint a picture in the reader's mind.

Example

Flames lick the sky
Hot and bright, orange and yellow
Dangerous but beautiful.

> This describes how flames move upwards, licking like tongues, and how fire can look beautiful despite being dangerous.

Understanding a poem

Read the whole poem to understand what it is about.

Example

Alone at sea.
Crossing over the ocean wide.
Storms and sun, no place to hide.
A scary, lonely, thrilling ride.
Alone at sea.
Nothing to see for miles around.
The wind and waves the only sound.
In my boat is where I'm found.
Alone at sea.

> 'wide', 'hide' and 'ride' all rhyme.

> The words 'Alone at sea' are recurring throughout.

> 'around', 'sound' and 'found' all rhyme.

The poem is about somebody in a boat on the ocean. It can be scary and lonely. All they have around them is the ocean. There is no shelter from storms and sun. 'Alone at sea' keeps recurring to remind the reader that the person in the boat is alone. It can help the reader imagine what that might feel like.

Remember

Think about what the words in a poem mean.

Tip

Read the whole poem and think about how it makes you feel. Discuss what the words mean.

Key words

- poem
- rhyme

Challenge 1

1. Read the poem and add words to rhyme with **cat** and **head**.

Oliver Jackson had a **cat**,
Which always wore a coloured _____,
Placed upon his furry **head**,
It was green and white with spots of _____.

2 marks

Challenge 2

1. Read the poem, then answer the questions.

If you go inside the big,
old house
It seems that no one's
living there.
But this is the home of
Milly Mouse
Who has a hole beneath
the stair.

Milly sleeps for most of
the day
But at night strolls from
room to room.
She eats and drinks and
likes to play
Before she sweeps up
with her broom.

a) Who is this poem about? _____

b) Which word is used to rhyme with stair? _____

c) What does the mouse do most of the day? _____

3 marks

Challenge 3

1. Read this short poem and answer the questions.

Slowly, the hot beast
Raises its long, grey trunk
Sprays water on its head and back
And smiles to itself.

b) Which **two** words describe the trunk?

_____

c) Why does it smile to itself?

_____

a) What is the 'beast' in this poem?

_____

3 marks

Total: ☐ /8 marks

Had a go ☐   **Getting there** ☐   **Got it!** ☐

Non-fiction

- Recognise key features of non-fiction texts
- Understand the meaning of new words

Non-fiction texts

A **non-fiction** text is **factual**. It tells us information about real things. **Instructions** and **explanations** are both types of non-fiction texts. Non-fiction texts have some common features.

Example

Icebergs ← title – what the text is about

Icebergs are very large pieces of ice floating in the sea. They break ← text explaining about icebergs
off from large ice sheets in the Arctic ← new words to learn about
and Antarctic.
Most of the iceberg cannot be seen
as it is below the water. Eventually icebergs
melt as they float into warmer waters.

A picture of an iceberg to help the reader to understand.

In 1912, a ship called *Titanic* hit an iceberg in the Atlantic Ocean. The ship sank and many lives were lost. ← fact box giving an interesting fact

Reading a non-fiction text like this can help you answer lots of questions, such as:
- Where do icebergs come from?
- How do icebergs melt?

Non-fiction texts give you information.

The words '**ice sheets**' are highlighted in the text above. Highlighted words in non-fiction books are often explained in a **glossary** at the end of the book.

Read this passage from a book called 'Zoo Life' and then answer the questions.

Amy is a zookeeper. She is responsible for the big cats. Each day, Amy must check on all the big cats. They all need feeding with fresh meat.

She checks that each animal is healthy. If a cat is injured or sick, she must help them. When a mother lion was ill, Amy fed the lion cubs by hand.

Amy enjoys her job but says it can be very hard when animals are sick.

Challenge 1

1. a) What two things does Amy do each day?

   _____

   b) What must Amy do if a creature is injured or sick?

   _____

   c) Why did Amy feed the lion cubs by hand?

   _____

   3 marks

Challenge 2

1. Tick the fact box that works best with the passage above. Explain your choice.

| Lots of people like cats. Some people like lions. | | Big cats is the name given to lions, tigers, leopards and cheetahs. | | Amy likes to play tennis in her spare time. | |

   _____

   2 marks

Challenge 3

1. The text says Amy is 'responsible for the big cats'. Explain what this means.

   _____

   1 mark

   Total: [　] /6 marks

Had a go [　] **Getting there** [　] **Got it!** [　]

Inference and prediction

- Make inferences based on what happens in the text
- Make predictions based on what has been read so far

What is happening in the text?

Making **inferences** means looking for clues in a text. Thinking about why a character acts in a certain way or how they might feel can develop your understanding.

Example

Tommy <u>had a big smile</u>. He was on his way to see his Grandma.

> The words 'had a big smile' help us to **infer** that Tommy was happy that he was going to visit his Grandma.

Jess <u>forced a smile</u>. She thanked her aunt for the new dress but <u>she knew she could never wear anything like that</u>.

> The words do not say that Jess disliked the dress but the underlined words infer this.

Tip

Thinking about why something happens helps you to understand the story.

What will happen in the text?

Prediction, or thinking about what will or might happen in a story, shows you have understood a text.

Example

Here is an extract from a story about an adventurer, Sam, who needs to get to a shelter to survive.

The path was long and covered in ice. A biting wind blew in her face. The safety of the shelter was still a long way off, meaning several more hours without water, food or sleep. Slowly, Sam put one foot in front of the other. There would be more challenges in the dark mountains, but she was determined.

> This last sentence may help to form your prediction.

From reading this extract, you might predict that Sam will eventually reach the shelter safely.

Key words

- inference
- prediction

Challenge 1

1. Draw a line from each action to say which feeling it shows. One has been done for you.

blubbing   shaking   smiling   trembling   grinning   tearful

happy   **sad**   **nervous**

5 marks

Challenge 2

1. Read the text and answer the question.

> Sam closed her eyes and bit her lip, determined **to ignore the pain** in her legs. The storm was still blowing and **she was in danger** but **she carried on despite her injuries**.

What do the highlighted words infer about Sam? Tick one.

She is scared. ☐   She is sad. ☐   She is brave. ☐

1 mark

Challenge 3

1. Read the text and answer the questions.

> The last part of the cake was tricky. Lena's hand was shaking a little as she slowly put the final piece of icing into place. She held her breath, her tongue sticking out a bit.
>
> Ever so carefully she moved her hand away, letting out a big breath and giving a little smile. At that moment, the judges entered the room to decide which was the best cake.

a) How do you think Lena is feeling? Which words tell you this?

_____

b) What do you think will happen next?

_____

2 marks

Total: ☐ /8 marks

Had a go ☐   **Getting there** ☐   **Got it!** ☐

Progress test I

1. **Circle the correct exception word to use in each sentence.**

   a) I wish I **cud / could** swim faster.

   b) We **would / wood** have all gone if we'd known.

   c) I **shud / should** have done my homework.

   3 marks

2. **In some words ending in -y, the y is removed before adding -ies. Write the root word for each of the words below.**

flies	copies	babies	replies	cries
_____	_____	_____	_____	_____

   5 marks

3. **Write 1, 2, 3 and 4 in the boxes to put the events in the correct order.**

Humpty fell.	They could not repair Humpty.	All the King's men came.	Humpty sat on a wall.
☐	☐	☐	☐

   4 marks

4. **Circle the word that has a similar meaning to the underlined word in each sentence.**

   a) The Prince <u>searched</u> for Cinderella.   **looked / cared**

   b) The wolf was <u>exhausted</u>.   **hungry / tired**

   c) Daddy Bear was <u>furious</u>.   **happy / angry**

   3 marks

5. Read the words. Circle the words that have an s sound as in 'sat'.

icy   call   capital   nice   city   cell   racing   club

6. Read the text from a book called 'Climbing High' and then answer the questions.

Saja is a climber. He has been rock climbing for eight years. Every weekend he visits the climbing wall for training. After his own training session, he coaches children.

Saja also takes part in competitions. He has numerous medals and trophies.

The sport is difficult and dangerous. Saja wears a helmet. He has to keep fit and strong and must be able to think carefully and quickly.

a) What two things does Saja do at the climbing wall?

_____

_____

b) What does the word 'numerous' mean?

_____

c) Which word tells you why Saja needs to wear a helmet?

_____

7. **Think about the sound the g makes in each word below and then write the words in the correct boxes.**

magic   gold   age   log   giant   change   huge   game

g as a j sound (as in jet)	g as a g sound (as in gum)

8 marks

8. **Read the text and answer the questions.**

It had been a long day at school. **Zara sat on the sofa and her eyes started to close.**

A loud knock on the door made Zara leap to her feet. Could this be the parcel she had been waiting for? Her heart pounded as she ran to the door. Mum was already there and was paying the window cleaner.

Zara sulkily walked back to the living room.

a) What does the highlighted sentence tell us about how Zara was feeling?

_____

b) What does the phrase 'leap to her feet' mean?

_____

c) Which word tells us that Zara was not happy? _____

3 marks

9. **Read the poem and then answer the questions.**

Rain lashes down,
Making rivers flow,
Watering the crops.

Sun follows later,
Helping plants grow,
Bringing warmth and life.

Soon the cold returns,
Ice, frost and snow,
As life stands still.

a) What does the word 'lashes' tell you about how it is raining? Circle one.

lightly   **gently**   **heavily**

b) In the poem, what does it say helps plants to grow? _____

c) What three things does the cold bring?

_____   _____   _____

d) Why do you think 'life stands still' at the end of the poem?

_____

6 marks

10. **Write down how many syllables each word has.**

a) computer

b) crayon

c) plant

d) incredible

4 marks

Total: [ ] / 45 marks

Counting forwards and backwards

- Count forwards and backwards in steps of 2, 3 and 5 from 0
- Count forwards and backwards in tens from any number

Counting in 2s, 3s and 5s from 0

When counting forwards in steps of 2, you add 2 each time. This is **repeated addition** of 2.

You can also do the opposite (the **inverse**) and count backwards in 2s. This is **repeated subtraction** of 2.

Example

Repeated addition of 2

0 1 2 3 4 5 6 7 8 9 10 11 12 13 14 15 16 17 18 19 20 21 22 23 24

Repeated subtraction of 2

Tip

Practise counting in 2s by missing out ONE number. Practise counting in 3s by missing out TWO numbers. Practise counting in 5s by missing out FOUR numbers.

Counting forwards in steps of 3 or 5 is **repeated addition of 3 or 5**. Counting backwards in 3s or 5s is **repeated subtraction of 3 or 5**.

Example

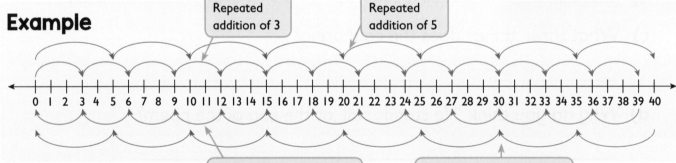

Repeated addition of 3   Repeated addition of 5

0 1 2 3 4 5 6 7 8 9 10 11 12 13 14 15 16 17 18 19 20 21 22 23 24 25 26 27 28 29 30 31 32 33 34 35 36 37 38 39 40

Repeated subtraction of 3   Repeated subtraction of 5

Counting in 10s

Look at the 100 square.

If you count forwards 10 from the number 36, you get 46. If you count backwards 10 from the number 36, you get 26.

If you count forwards 10 from the number 72, you get 82. If you count backwards 10 from the number 72, you get 62.

1	2	3	4	5	6	7	8	9	10
11	12	13	14	15	16	17	18	19	20
21	22	23	24	25	26	27	28	29	30
31	32	33	34	35	36	37	38	39	40
41	42	43	44	45	46	47	48	49	50
51	52	53	54	55	56	57	58	59	60
61	62	63	64	65	66	67	68	69	70
71	72	73	74	75	76	77	78	79	80
81	82	83	84	85	86	87	88	89	90
91	92	93	94	95	96	97	98	99	100

Key words

- repeated addition
- inverse
- repeated subtraction

Challenge 1

1. Fill in the missing numbers on the number lines.

```
←——┼——┼——┼——┼——┼——┼——[ ]——┼——┼——┼——[ ]——┼——┼——→
    0   2   4   6   8  10      14  16  18      22  24
```

```
←——┼——┼——┼——┼——┼——[ ]——┼——┼——[ ]——┼——┼——┼——┼——→
    0   3   6   9  12      18  21      27  30  33  36
```

[ ] 4 marks

Challenge 2

Look at the sequences. Continue the sequences by writing the next 3 numbers.

1. a) 24, 22, 20, [ ], [ ], [ ]

   b) 33, 30, 27, [ ], [ ], [ ]

   c) 55, 50, 45, [ ], [ ], [ ]

   d) 91, 81, 71, [ ], [ ], [ ]

2. a) 4, 6, 8, [ ], [ ], [ ]

   b) 12, 15, 18, [ ], [ ], [ ]

   c) 25, 30, 35, [ ], [ ], [ ]

   d) 34, 44, 54, [ ], [ ], [ ]

[ ] 8 marks

Challenge 3

1. Read the sentences and write down the number you get to. Use the number lines on the opposite page to help you.

   a) Start at 16 and count forwards 3 jumps of 2. [ ]

   b) Start at 21 and count backwards 2 jumps of 3. [ ]

   c) Start at 35 and count forwards 4 jumps of 5. [ ]

   d) Start at 51 and count backwards 4 jumps of 10. [ ]

[ ] 4 marks

Total: [ ] / 16 marks

Had a go [ ]   Getting there [ ]   Got it! [ ]

27

The value of digits

- Recognise the place value of each digit in a 2-digit number

What does place value mean?

You can tell the **place value** of a **digit** by looking at where it is placed within the number.

Example

A single-digit number such as 3 has a value of 3 ones.

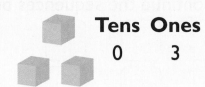

Tens	Ones
0	3

When a number gets above 9, it contains at least one **ten** and so it is a 2-digit number.

Example

A 2-digit number such as 34 has a total value of 3 tens and 4 ones.

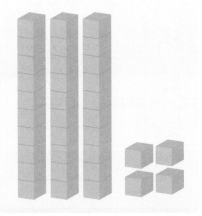

Tens	Ones
3	4

Column number system

When writing the number 34, the 3 is in the 'tens' column and the 4 is in the 'ones' column.

Tens	Ones
3	4

This is the **column number system**

When you split a number into each digit's value, it is called **partitioning**. The 3 in the number 34 is not just 3; it is worth 30. It is 3 tens. The 4 ones is just 4 ones. So, 34 is really 30 and 4 (**34 = 30 + 4**).

When you put a number back together, it is called **recombining**: 30 + 4 = 34

Remember

9 is the biggest number that can go in any column.

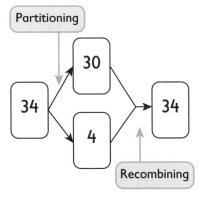

Partitioning

34 → 30, 4 → 34

Recombining

Key words

- place value
- digit
- column number system
- partitioning
- recombining

Challenge 1

1. Each picture shows a number. Write the number in the box.

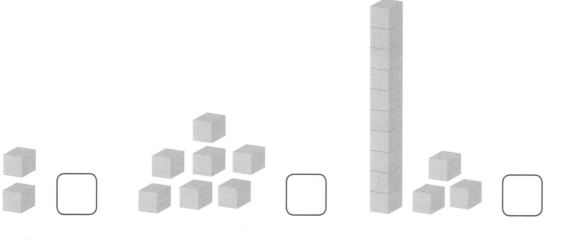

Challenge 2

1. How many ones are there in these numbers?

a) 13 = ☐ ones   b) 24 = ☐ ones   c) 46 = ☐ ones

2. How many tens are there in these numbers?

a) 13 = ☐ tens   b) 24 = ☐ tens   c) 46 = ☐ tens

Challenge 3

1. Add the numbers in words together and write your answer in numerals (figures).

seventy + five = ☐   ninety + one = ☐   thirty + three = ☐

PS 2. Fill in the missing numbers.

50 + ☐ = 54   20 + ☐ = 29   30 + ☐ = 35

Total: ☐ / 15 marks

Had a go ☐   **Getting there** ☐   **Got it!** ☐

Comparing numbers

- Compare and order numbers from 0 to 100
- Use the <, > and = signs

More and less

Comparing numbers simply means finding what is different about them.

Each number has a value. Bigger means a **higher number value**. Smaller means a **lower number value**. A number that has a higher value is further up the number sequence. A number that has a lower value is further down the number sequence.

1 2 3 4 5 6 7 8 9 10

> 2 has a lower value than 8 so it is further down the number sequence.

Remember

Numbers can be compared using words such as bigger, higher, more than, smaller, lower, less than, equal to.

>, < and = signs

- The symbol < means 'is less than'.
- The symbol > means 'is more than'.
- The symbol = means 'is equal to'.

Tip

Imagine the arrows (> and <) are like the mouth of a crocodile. The open 'mouth' always eats the greater value.

> <

Example

11 < 20	11 is less than 20
38 > 29	38 is more than 29
50 = 50	50 is equal to 50

Ordering numbers

Once you know the **value** of a number, you can **compare** it to other numbers. When you can compare the numbers, you can **order** them.

Example

These numbers are in order from smallest to biggest:

7, 18, 21, 33, 37, 40

> 18 is greater than 7 because it has more tens

These numbers are in order from biggest to smallest:

40, 37, 33, 21, 18, 7

> 37 is greater than 33 because it has more ones

Key word

- ordering

Challenge 1

1. Write the correct phrase in between the numbers.

more than	less than	equal to

a) 3 is _____ 9

b) 8 is _____ 1

c) 10 is _____ 10

3 marks

Challenge 2

1. Complete the sentences by choosing numbers from the list below.

9   2   4   5   7   10   1   8   5   3   6

a) ☐ is less than ☐   b) ☐ is more than ☐

c) ☐ is less than ☐   d) ☐ is more than ☐

4 marks

2. Order the numbers from smallest to biggest:

4   28   7   1   18

☐   ☐   ☐   ☐   ☐

Smallest   **Biggest**

5 marks

Challenge 3

1. Use the symbols **<** (less than), **>** (greater than) and **=** (equal to) to compare the numbers.

a) 23 ☐ 23

b) 38 ☐ 41

c) 57 ☐ 50

>, < =

d) 61 ☐ 68

4 marks

Total: ☐ / 16 marks

Had a go ☐   **Getting there** ☐   **Got it!** ☐

Numbers to 100

- Read and write numbers to at least 100 in numerals and in words
- Estimate numbers on a number line

Numbers and words

Numbers are sometimes written as words, so it is important that you know how to read and write numbers as words.

Look at the tables below. Any number up to 100 can be made from the words below.

1	2	3	4	5	6	7	8	9	10
one	two	three	four	five	six	seven	eight	nine	ten

11	12	13	14	15	16	17	18	19	20
eleven	twelve	thirteen	fourteen	fifteen	sixteen	seventeen	eighteen	nineteen	twenty

30	40	50	60	70	80	90	100
thirty	forty	fifty	sixty	seventy	eighty	ninety	one hundred

> **Remember**
>
> A numeral is how we write a number, and a number means the amount for a numeral. This means they are the same.

> **Tip**
>
> When writing the words for numbers, use the 'look, say, cover, write, check' method to learn the spellings.

Estimating numbers on a number line

Estimating means having a good guess at something, using facts that you already know.

Example

Look at this **number line**. There are only two numbers: 0 and 10. Now look at where the arrow is. What number could it be pointing at?

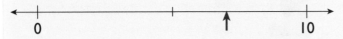

You already know that half of 10 is 5 and that 1, 2, 3 and 4 come before 5 so the answer can't be 1, 2, 3, 4, or 5. It must be between 5 and 10 so a good estimate would be 6 or 7.

> **Key words**
>
> - estimate
> - number line

Challenge 1

1. Complete the table. For each set of objects, write the numeral and word. Look at the study page for help with spelling the words.

Numeral	Objects	Word
	⬤⬤⬤⚪⚪⬤ ⬤⬤⚪⚪⬤	
	⬜⬜⬜⬜⬜⬛ ⬜⬜⬜⬜ ⬜⬜⬜⬜	

4 marks

Challenge 2

1. Here is a number chart. Some of the numerals and words are missing. Fill in the missing numerals and words.

	28		39	
twenty-five	_____	thirty-one	_____	forty-one

	80		91	
seventy-two	_____	eighty-nine	_____	one hundred

10 marks

Challenge 3

1. Estimate the number that the arrow is pointing to on these number lines.

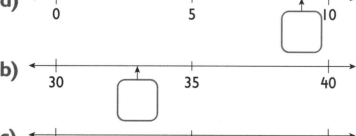

a) 0   5   10

b) 30   35   40

c) 70   80   90

3 marks

Total: ☐ / 17 marks

Had a go ☐   **Getting there** ☐   **Got it!** ☐

Number facts

- Recall and use addition facts to 20
- Use related facts up to 100

Number facts

A **number fact** (**number bond**) is a pair of numbers that equals an amount. Lots of different pairs of numbers can equal the same amount.

Example

There are lots of ways to make 20. Here are the number bonds to 20:

$0 + 20$, $1 + 19$, $2 + 18$, $3 + 17$, $4 + 16$, $5 + 15$, $6 + 14$, $7 + 13$, $8 + 12$, $9 + 11$, $10 + 10$, $11 + 9$, $12 + 8$, $13 + 7$, $14 + 6$, $15 + 5$, $16 + 4$, $17 + 3$, $18 + 2$, $19 + 1$, $20 + 0$

Number facts to 100

When finding number facts to 100, you can use number facts to 10, and place value together. This is done by moving the digits into the tens column, and then filling in the space in the ones column with a '0'.

Example

$7 + 3 = 10$, therefore $70 + 30 = 100$

When you know the number facts to 10 and 20, it is easier to work out the facts to 100.

Example

What goes with 64 to make 100? ($64 + ? = 100$)

You know that $4 + 6 = 10$, so the **ones** part of the answer must end in **6**. Now add that **6** to **64** to get **70**. From 70, you need to add **30** to reach **100** so the **tens** part of the answer must be a **3**.
$64 + 36 = 100$

> **Tip**
>
> Knowing number facts to 10 and 20 makes it easier to calculate facts to 100.

> Here is a **fact family** for one fact for the number 20:
>
> **Addition:** $1 + 19 = 20$ and $19 + 1 = 20$
> **Subtraction:** $20 - 1 = 19$ and $20 - 19 = 1$

> **Remember**
>
> When you see the 'place holder 0' at the end of a number, it means it has been multiplied by 10.

> **Key words**
>
> - number facts
> - number bonds
> - addition
> - subtraction

Challenge 1

1. Complete the number bonds to 20.

   a) 1 + ☐ = 20   ☐ + 0 = 20   2 + ☐ = 20   3 + ☐ = 20

   b) 19 + ☐ = 20   ☐ + 10 = 20   12 + ☐ = 20   17 + ☐ = 20

2. Complete the number sentences.

   a) 20 – ☐ = 10   20 – ☐ = 1   20 – ☐ = 18   20 – ☐ = 15

   b) 20 – ☐ = 13   20 – ☐ = 17   20 – ☐ = 14   20 – ☐ = 4

   ☐ 16 marks

Challenge 2

PS 1. Complete the number sentences.

   30 + ☐ = 100   100 – ☐ = 45   62 + ☐ = 100   100 – ☐ = 87

PS 2. Complete the bar models by filling in the missing numbers to total 100.

   a)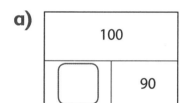

   b)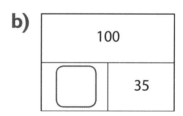

   ☐ 6 marks

Challenge 3

PS 1. Use **+** or **–** to complete the number sentences.

   a) 10 ☐ 90 = 100   100 ☐ 40 = 60

   b) 12 ☐ 88 = 100   100 ☐ 25 = 75

   c) 30 ☐ 70 = 100   5 ☐ 95 = 100

   ☐ 6 marks

Total: ☐ / 28 marks

Had a go ☐   **Getting there** ☐   **Got it!** ☐

35

Addition and subtraction

- Add and subtract ones and tens from 2-digit numbers
- Add and subtract 2-digit numbers from 2-digit numbers

Adding and subtracting

Always start with the larger number and count on **forwards** for **addition** or **backwards** for **subtraction** with the smaller number.

$26 + 5 =$

Example

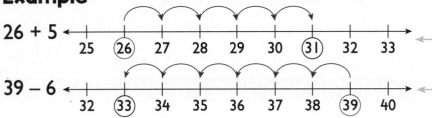

26 + 5

39 – 6

26 is the larger number so start at 26 and count on 5 jumps: $26 + 5 = 31$

39 is the larger number so start at 39 and count back 6 jumps: $39 - 6 = 33$

Adding and subtracting tens

When adding or subtracting 10, the **ones** part of the answer always stays the same. (Look back at page 26.)

Example

The number 56 has 5 tens and 6 ones. If you add 10 you get **66**. If you subtract 10 you get **46**.

Adding and subtracting 2-digit numbers

Example

34 + 21

- Partition the smaller number 21 into **20** and **1**
- Now, add 34 and 20, which equals 54
- Finally, add the 1 to get **55**

67 – 33

- Partition the smaller number, 33, into **30** and **3**
- Now, subtract 30 from 67, which equals 37
- Finally, subtract the 3 to get **34**

Remember

To check your answer, carry out the **inverse** (opposite) operation.

Tip

Estimate what you think the answer could be and use facts that you already know.

Key words

- addition
- subtraction
- inverse

Challenge 1

1. Use the number line to complete the calculation. Write the answer in the box.

78 + 9 = ☐

2. Use the number line to complete the calculation. Write the answer in the box.

44 − 7 = ☐

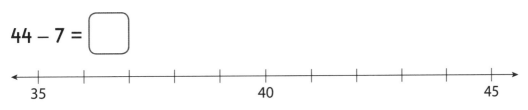

☐
2 marks

Challenge 2

1. Complete the calculations. Write the answer in the box.

36 + 10 = ☐   78 + 20 = ☐

2. Complete the calculations. Write the answer in the box.

44 − 10 = ☐   81 − 30 = ☐

☐
4 marks

Challenge 3

1. Use partitioning and adding on to complete the calculations. Write the answer in the box.

34 + 21 = ☐   46 + 35 = ☐

2. Use partitioning and counting back to complete the calculations. Write the answer in the box.

77 − 19 = ☐   96 − 12 = ☐

☐
4 marks

Total: ☐ / 10 marks

Had a go ☐   Getting there ☐   Got it! ☐

Adding single-digit numbers

- Add three single-digit numbers

Single-digit (1-digit) numbers

A single-digit number has just one digit. In **place value**, they belong to the **ones** column.

Often when adding numbers, two amounts are added together, e.g. 5 + 6. But you need to be able to add three amounts together, e.g. 6 + 3 + 5.

Example

The numbers 6 + 3 + 5 can be added in any order, but it's easiest to add the two largest numbers first:

6 + 5 ← When the amount of **ones** goes past 9, a **ten** is made, with one left over. This is 11.

Then add the remaining, smallest number: **11 + 3**

11 + 3 = 14

Using number bonds and doubles

A quick way to add three single-digit numbers is to see if there is a **number bond** between two numbers. If there are two numbers that are the same, this can be worked out as a **double** (see page 44).

Example

Here is 8 + 7 + 2
This addition includes 8 and 2, which is a number bond to 10: **8 + 2 = 10**

Then **add** the remaining number: **10 + 7 = 17**

Here is 4 + 3 + 4. Notice that there are two 4s.
Double 4 = 8. Finally add the 3: **8 + 3 = 11**

Remember

A single-digit number is a 1-digit number. This means it is just one numeral. The numbers 0, 1, 2, 3, 4, 5, 6, 7, 8, and 9 are all single-digit numbers.

Tip

When there are three single-digit amounts, try to find number facts to 10, or try to find doubles.

Key words

- place value
- number bonds

Challenge 1

1. Write the totals of these numbers. Use the same numbers to write two different calculations.

a)

$\boxed{} + \boxed{} + \boxed{} = \boxed{}$

$\boxed{} + \boxed{} + \boxed{} = \boxed{}$

b)

$\boxed{} + \boxed{} + \boxed{} = \boxed{}$

$\boxed{} + \boxed{} + \boxed{} = \boxed{}$

$\boxed{}$ 4 marks

Challenge 2

1. Which **three** numbers add up to **12**? Circle three numbers.

    4   6   9   2   3   5

2. Which **three** numbers add up to **18**? Circle three numbers.

    4   6   7   7   3   2

3. Which **three** numbers add up to **21**? Circle three numbers.

    1   5   7   4   8   9

$\boxed{}$ 3 marks

Challenge 3

PS 1. James has 4 marbles. Rita has double the number of James's marbles.
   Rose has 3 marbles.
   How many marbles do the children have in total? $\boxed{}$

2. Rita has 6 apples. James has 9 apples. Rose has 4 apples.
   How many apples do the children have in total?
   Show this in three different addition sums.

$\boxed{}$ 4 marks

Total: $\boxed{}$ / 11 marks

Had a go $\boxed{}$ Getting there $\boxed{}$ Got it! $\boxed{}$

39

Multiplication, commutativity and odds and evens

- Recall and use multiplication facts for the 2, 5 and 10 times tables
- Show that multiplication of two numbers can be done in any order
- Recognise odd and even numbers

Multiplication

Multiplication means **lots of**, or times. It is **repeated addition**: adding the same number lots of times.
Multiplication is an **operation** and is shown by the symbol **x**.
Multiplication can be represented by pictures or objects arranged in rows and columns, called an **array**.

Example

This array shows the multiplication **4 x 2**

There are four columns, with two circles in each column. There are 8 circles in total.

4 x 2 = 8 is the same as 2 + 2 + 2 + 2 = 8

Numbers that are multiplied are called **factors**. The answer is called the **product**. In the example above, 4 and 2 are the factors, and 8 is the product.

Commutativity

A multiplication using two numbers can be done in any order and still have the same answer. This means multiplication is **commutative**. 4 x 2 = 8, but also 2 x 4 = 8. It doesn't matter which way round the **factors** are multiplied, the answer (**product**) remains the same.

2, 5 and 10 times tables

This grid shows the 2, 5 and 10 times tables, up to 12.
Try to learn them.

	x 1	x 2	x 3	x 4	x 5	x 6	x 7	x 8	x 9	x 10	x 11	x 12
2		4	6	8	10	12	14	16	18	20	22	24
5		10	15	20	25	30	35	40	45	50	55	60
10		20	30	40	50	60	70	80	90	100	110	120

Remember

All the answers in the 2 and 10 times tables are even. For the 5 times table, all answers end in either 0 or 5 (those that end in 0 are even).

Tip

Practise learning times tables in different ways, e.g. chanting or singing them, or using online games.

Key words

- multiplication
- repeated addition
- operation
- array
- factor
- product
- commutativity

Challenge 1

1. Look at the arrays and write a multiplication sentence for each.

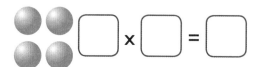 $\boxed{} \times \boxed{} = \boxed{}$ 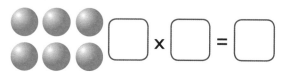 $\boxed{} \times \boxed{} = \boxed{}$

2. Look at the array and complete two multiplication sentences.

   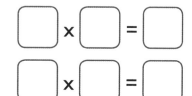

$\boxed{} \times \boxed{} = \boxed{}$

$\boxed{} \times \boxed{} = \boxed{}$

4 marks

Challenge 2

1. Continue the numbers in each sequence.

a) 12,   14, $\boxed{}$, $\boxed{}$, $\boxed{}$

b) 35,   40, $\boxed{}$, $\boxed{}$, $\boxed{}$

c) 80,   90, $\boxed{}$, $\boxed{}$, $\boxed{}$

3 marks

Challenge 3

1. Complete the table.

Repeated addition	Multiplication sentence 1	Multiplication sentence 2
2 + 2 + 2 = 6		2 x 3 = 6
3 + 3 + 3 + 3 + 3	3 x 5 = 15	
		2 x 2 = 4
2 + 2 + 2 + 2 = 8		4 x 2 = 8
	5 x 5 = 25	
9 + 9 + 9 + 9 + 9 + 9 + 9 + 9 + 9 + 9 = 90	9 x 10 = 90	

8 marks

Total: $\boxed{}$ / 15 marks

Had a go $\boxed{}$ Getting there $\boxed{}$ Got it! $\boxed{}$

Sharing, grouping and division facts

- Recall and use division facts for the 2, 5 and 10 times tables
- Calculate mathematical statements for division
- Recognise odd and even numbers

Division

Division means to share into equal amounts or split into groups containing the same amount. Division is an operation. It is shown by the symbol ÷.

Sharing and grouping

- When you divide by **sharing**, you share out the larger number equally between groups. The answer is how many are in each group.
- When you divide by **grouping**, you split the larger number into groups of the same amount. The answer is how many groups there are.

Example

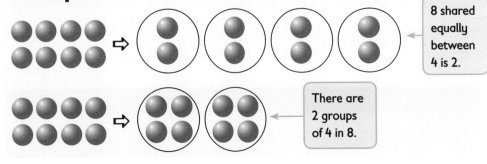

8 shared equally between 4 is 2.

There are 2 groups of 4 in 8.

Division facts

- Division is the opposite, or **inverse**, of multiplication.
- Division is **repeated subtraction**: the total amount is shared or grouped into smaller amounts.
- For each multiplication fact, there is another multiplication fact, *and* two division facts.

Example

For the multiplication fact 4 × 2 = 8,
- there is another multiplication fact: 2 × 4 = 8
- and two division facts: 8 ÷ 4 = 2 and 8 ÷ 2 = 4

Remember

Odd numbers cannot be divided equally into whole numbers. Only even numbers can be divided equally.

Remember

Always divide the larger number by the smaller number.

Tip

Use multiplication to check your answer for division. Use division to check your answer for multiplication.

Key words

- division
- even numbers
- odd numbers
- whole number
- inverse
- repeated subtraction

Challenge 1

1. Complete the bar model by filling in the missing numbers to show how the top number can be shared equally. Work these out with objects if needed.

a)

12

b)

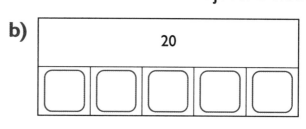

20

2 marks

2. Group the spots in the arrays, then complete the number sentences.

a) Draw circles around each group of 6.

$12 \div \boxed{} = \boxed{}$

b) Draw circles around each group of 4.

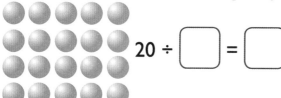

$20 \div \boxed{} = \boxed{}$

2 marks

Challenge 2

1. Here are 20 beads. How can you share 20 equally between 2, 5 and 10?

20 shared between 2 equals $\boxed{}$

20 shared between 5 equals $\boxed{}$

20 shared between 10 equals $\boxed{}$

3 marks

Challenge 3

1. Look at the multiplication sentences. Complete two division sentences for each.

a) $8 \times 5 = 40$ $\boxed{} \div \boxed{} = \boxed{}$ $\boxed{} \div \boxed{} = \boxed{}$

b) $11 \times 2 = 22$ $\boxed{} \div \boxed{} = \boxed{}$ $\boxed{} \div \boxed{} = \boxed{}$

c) $9 \times 10 = 90$ $\boxed{} \div \boxed{} = \boxed{}$ $\boxed{} \div \boxed{} = \boxed{}$

6 marks

Total: $\boxed{}$ / 13 marks

Had a go $\boxed{}$	Getting there $\boxed{}$	Got it! $\boxed{}$

Doubling and halving

- Relate multiplication and division to doubling and halving

Doubling

When you multiply any number by 2, you **double** its value. Doubling can be shown by writing **x 2**, which means there are two groups of an amount. Any number can be doubled, and the answer will always be an **even number** (the last digit will end in 0, 2, 4, 6 or 8).

When doubling 2-digit numbers, it is helpful to **partition** into tens and ones and then **recombine** them.

Example

Double the number 13.

| Partition 13 into tens and ones to get 10 and 3. |
| Double 10 to get 20, and double 3 to get 6. |
| Add 20 and 6 to find the total of 26. |

13
1 (ten)   3 (ones)
↓   ↓
doubled   doubled
↓   ↓
2 (tens)   6 (ones)

Halving

When you divide any number by 2, you **halve** its value. Halving can be shown by writing ÷ **2**, which means splitting the total amount into two equal groups.

Odd numbers (ending in 1, 3, 5, 7 and 9) cannot be divided in **half** to give whole numbers.

When halving 2-digit numbers, it is helpful to partition into tens and ones and then recombine half of the number.

Example

Halve the number 18.

| Partition 18 into tens and ones to get 10 and 8. |
| Halve 10 to get 5. Halve 8 to get 4. |
| Add 5 and 4 to find the total of 9. |

18
1 (ten)   8 (ones)
↓   ↓
halved   halved
↓   ↓
5 (ones)   4 (ones)

Key words

- even numbers
- partitioning
- recombining
- odd numbers
- half

Challenge 1

1. Count the spots. Double the spots by drawing the same number of spots again. Complete the number sentence to show the double.

    2 x ⬜ = ⬜

    2 x ⬜ = ⬜

2. Draw a circle around half of the spots. Complete the number sentence to show the half.

⬜ ÷ 2 = ⬜

3 marks

Challenge 2

1. Double each number by partitioning and recombining.

a) 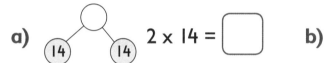 14 14   2 x 14 = ⬜   b) 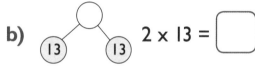 13 13   2 x 13 = ⬜

2. Halve each number by partitioning and combining two of the halves.

a) 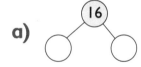 16   16 ÷ 2 = ⬜   b) 18   18 ÷ 2 = ⬜

4 marks

Challenge 3

1. Add the place value cards and then double them. Complete the number sentences.

a) 10 1   2 x ⬜ = ⬜   b) 20 4   2 x ⬜ = ⬜

PS 2. Complete the sentences.

a) Nine is half, so the whole is ⬜.

b) Thirteen is half, so the whole is ⬜.

4 marks

Total: ⬜ / 11 marks

Had a go ⬜   **Getting there** ⬜   **Got it!** ⬜

45

Progress test 2

1. Continue each sequence by writing the next 3 numbers.

   a) 14, 12, 10, ☐ , ☐ , ☐

   b) 15, 12, 9, ☐ , ☐ , ☐

   c) 45, 40, 35, ☐ , ☐ , ☐

   d) 73, 63, 53, ☐ , ☐ , ☐

   ☐ 4 marks

2. Order the numbers from smallest to biggest.

   15   8   68   90   31

   ☐   ☐   ☐   ☐   ☐

   Smallest   **Biggest**

   ☐ 1 mark

3. Look at the picture. Complete two multiplication sentences.

   ☐ x ☐ = ☐   ☐ x ☐ = ☐

   ☐ 2 marks

4. Using these three number cards, make three different 2-digit numbers.

   2   6   9

   ☐   ☐   ☐

   ☐ 3 marks

46

5. Circle three numbers that add up to 19.

6   7   1   9   2   10

1 mark

6. Add the numbers in words together and write the answers in numerals.

thirty + five = ☐   eighty + two = ☐   fifty + one = ☐

3 marks

7. Circle two numbers that add up to 100.

60   70   20   90   30   100

1 mark

8. Continue each sequence by writing the next 3 numbers.

a) 0, 2, 4, ☐ , ☐ , ☐

b) 21, 24, 27, ☐ , ☐ , ☐

c) 35, 40, 45, ☐ , ☐ , ☐

d) 47, 57, 67, ☐ , ☐ , ☐

4 marks

PS 9. Nihal has 25 1p coins. How many 5p coins could he have instead of 25 1p coins?

☐

1 mark

10. Look at the array.

a) How many balls are in the array? ☐

b) Double the number ☐ x ☐ = ☐

c) Halve the number ☐ ÷ ☐ = ☐

3 marks

47

11. Circle the numbers that have a digit with a value of thirty.

3   8   14   18   30   37   53

1 mark

12. a) Write the number seventy in numerals.

☐

b) Write the number 64 in words.

_____

2 marks

13. Class A collect £69 from a school business project and Class B collect £29. How much did they collect altogether?

£ ☐

1 mark

14. Amara has 8 apples. Jack has 7 apples. Eve has 9 apples.
How many apples do the children have in total?
Show the calculation as three different addition sums.

☐ + ☐ + ☐ = ☐   ☐ + ☐ + ☐ = ☐

☐ + ☐ + ☐ = ☐

3 marks

15. Here is a number sentence: 38 + 56 = 94
Use this fact to complete three more facts.

☐ + ☐ = ☐   ☐ − ☐ = ☐   ☐ − ☐ = ☐

3 marks

16. Complete the following calculations.

a) 12 x 2 = ☐   10 x 5 = ☐   7 x 10 = ☐

b) 10 ÷ 2 = ☐   55 ÷ 5 = ☐   90 ÷ 10 = ☐

6 marks

17. Look at the picture. Complete two multiplication sentences.

$\boxed{}$ x $\boxed{}$ = $\boxed{}$ $\boxed{}$ x $\boxed{}$ = $\boxed{}$ $\boxed{}$

2 marks

PS 18. James bought 25 new toy monsters from the shop. He now has 70. How many did he have before?

$\boxed{}$

1 mark

19. Put the < or > or = sign between these numbers.

a) 6 tens and 5 ones $\boxed{}$ 56

b) eighty-eight $\boxed{}$ 88

c) 19 $\boxed{}$ 91

3 marks

20. Fill in the missing number on this number line.

25 26 27 28 29 30 31 32 33 34 $\boxed{}$ 36 37 38 39 40

$\boxed{}$

1 mark

21. There are 100 children in an infant school. It is sports day and the teachers put all the children into teams of 10. How many teams will there be?

$\boxed{}$

1 mark

22. There are 9 children who want to go out and play. They all put their wellies on. How many individual wellies are there altogether?

$\boxed{}$

1 mark

$\boxed{}$

Total: $\boxed{}$ / 48 marks

49

Handwriting

- Use diagonal and horizontal strokes to join letters

Cursive writing

As your handwriting develops, you can begin to use **cursive** writing to join letters.

Example

because

again

sugar

sure

> With cursive writing, the letters flow (connect) together.

Before using cursive writing, it is important to practise the joins. These are the diagonal and horizontal strokes that link the letters together. It is best to practise writing the individual letters.

Each of these letters starts at the red dot and finishes at the black dot. The arrows show the direction to follow to correctly form the letters.

Remember

When writing, make sure you are sitting correctly at a table, holding your pencil comfortably and correctly.

Tip

Practise the individual letters many times to make sure you keep a consistent size.

Key word

- cursive

Challenge 1

1. Trace over each of the letters.

a b c d e f g h i j k

l m n o p q r s t u v

w x y z

26 marks

Challenge 2

1. Copy each of the letters from Challenge 1, remembering to keep each letter the same size as the letter you are copying.

26 marks

Challenge 3

1. Copy each word below twice with the letters joined.

behind

who

because

fox

4 marks

Total: /56 marks

Had a go **Getting there** **Got it!**

Spelling sounds and homophones

- Segment spoken words into sounds and represent these sounds by letters
- Learn new ways of spelling sounds, including some that appear in common homophones
- Use compound words

Segmenting words

Segmenting a word means breaking it up into its separate sounds. These sounds are written as letters.

Example

Say the word 'chopping', breaking it up into one sound at a time:

ch – o – pp – i – ng

Some **common exception words** (such as: because, sugar, sure, behind, who, whole, beautiful, busy) cannot be segmented easily to help with spelling. You just have to learn how to spell these words.

> **Remember**
>
> Segmenting a word into its sounds can help you with spelling.

Homophones

Homophones are words that sound the same or nearly the same but have different spellings and meanings.

Example

there / their / they're	here / hear
bare / bear	blue / blew
night / knight	see / sea

> The words in each set sound the same but are spelt differently and mean different things.

Compound words

Some words are made by putting two words together.

Example

playground, bedroom, farmyard, football

To spell **compound words**, think about the spelling of each individual word before putting them together.

> **Key words**
>
> - segmenting
> - common exception word
> - homophone
> - compound word

Challenge 1

1. Segment the words below into their individual sounds. (It will help to say them out loud first.)

shoot _____   wrapping _____

cattle _____   knock _____

Challenge 2

1. Circle the correct homophone in each sentence.

a) The **night / knight** had a sword.

b) I sent **two / too** letters today.

c) Let's **meat / meet** at 3 o'clock.

d) **There / Their** lunch is ready.

e) I saw a **deer / dear** in the woods.

Challenge 3

1. Look at each of the common exception words below. Explain why each is a tricky word.

a) because _____

b) beautiful _____

2. Add another word to each of these words to make compound words.

a) blue_____

b) back_____

c) rain_____

d) tea_____

Total: ☐ / 15 marks

Had a go ☐   **Getting there** ☐   **Got it!** ☐

53

Using the apostrophe

- Use the apostrophe in words with contracted forms
- Use the possessive apostrophe

Contractions

A **contraction** is when two words are pushed together to make a shorter word. An **apostrophe** is a punctuation mark that shows where the missing letter or letters would be.

Example

I will ⇨ **Iwill** ⇨ **I'll**

> **I** and **will** can be pushed together to make I'll. The apostrophe shows that the letters 'wi' are missing.

There are many other contractions, including:

cannot ⇨ can't	she is ⇨ she's	has not ⇨ hasn't
could not ⇨ couldn't	it is ⇨ it's	did not ⇨ didn't

Remember

The missing letters in a contraction are replaced by the apostrophe.

Apostrophes to show belonging

The apostrophe is also used to show who, or what, something **belongs** to. This is known as **possession**.

Example

the dog's bone

> The apostrophe shows that the bone belongs to the dog.

my sister's bike

> The apostrophe shows that the bike belongs to my sister.

The teacher's car = the car belonging to the teacher

The car's wheels = the wheels belonging to the car

Raj's clothes = the clothes belonging to Raj

James's house = the house belonging to James

Key words

- contraction
- apostrophe
- possession

Challenge 1

1. Circle the correct contraction to replace the underlined words in each sentence.

   a) They <u>could not</u> find the keys.   **couldn't / could'nt**

   b) <u>I will</u> be waiting by the car.   **I'will / I'll**

   c) <u>She is</u> not being kind.   **She'is / She's**

   d) She <u>cannot</u> eat nuts.   **ca'nt / can't**

   4 marks

Challenge 2

1. Read the sentences below and then write the underlined word with an apostrophe to show possession.

   a) This is my <u>mums</u> car.   _____

   b) The <u>dogs</u> owners are Milo and Pippa.   _____

   c) On Fridays, we go to <u>Zaks</u> house.   _____

   d) <u>Noahs</u> dad drives buses.   _____

   4 marks

Challenge 3

1. Read the text below. Where words can be made into contractions, write the contraction. Where words require a possessive apostrophe, write the word with the apostrophe.

   Next week, I cannot go swimming because I   _____

   have to visit my friends farm in Wales.   _____

   It is a long journey and will take seven hours.   _____

   We are going to help feed Daisys new lambs.   _____

   _____

   5 marks

   Total: ☐ / 13 marks

Had a go ☐   **Getting there** ☐   **Got it!** ☐

Adding suffixes

- Add the suffixes -ing, -ed, -er, -est and -y to words
- Add the suffixes -ment, -ness, -ful, -less and -ly to words

Adding -ing, -ed, -er, -est and -y

Some **root words** keep the same spelling when adding a **suffix**. But:

- When adding a suffix to a one-syllable word that has a single consonant after a single vowel, the final consonant is doubled before adding the suffix
- For words ending in **-e** with a consonant before it, the **e** is removed before adding the suffix:

Example

hum ⇨ hum**ming**   drop ⇨ drop**ped**

big ⇨ big**g**er   thin ⇨ thin**n**est   fat ⇨ fat**t**y

hike ⇨ hik**ing**   shine ⇨ shin**y**   nice ⇨ nic**est**

> **Remember**
>
> An **adjective** is a describing word such as **big** or **small**. An **adverb** such as **quickly** or **carefully**, describes how something is being done.

> Final consonant is doubled before adding suffix.

> The **e** is removed before adding the suffix.

Adding -ment, -ness, -ful, -less and -ly

Usually, no change is needed to the root word before adding **-ment, -ness, -ful, -less** or **-ly**. But if the root word ends in a **consonant** followed by **y**, the **y** is replaced with **i** before the suffix is added.

Example

sad ⇨ sad**ness**   care ⇨ care**ful**   hope ⇨ hope**less**

happy ⇨ happ**i**ness   merry ⇨ merr**i**ment

happy ⇨ happ**ily**   plenty ⇨ plent**iful**

> No change is needed

> The **y** is replaced with **i** before the suffix is added.

Adding **-ly** can turn an **adjective** (a describing word) into an **adverb** (a word which describes *how* something is being done).

Example

adjective	adverb	adjective	adverb

quiet ⇨ quiet**ly**   merry ⇨ merr**ily**

> **Key words**
>
> - root word
> - suffix
> - adjective
> - adverb

1. Read each of the words below and then write the root word.

running _____ nicest _____

hopeless _____ happiness _____

patted _____ thoughtful _____

6 marks

Challenge 2

1. Explain how the ending of these words has changed when a suffix has been added.

hike ⇨ hiker   **bite ⇨ biting**   **smile ⇨ smiling**

_____

1 mark

Challenge 3

1. Explain the rule for adding the suffix for each word below.

a) run   ⇨   runner

_____

_____

b) happy   ⇨   happily

_____

_____

2 marks

Total: ☐ /9 marks

Had a go ☐   **Getting there** ☐   **Got it!** ☐

Writing fiction

- Write narratives about your own personal experiences and those of others
- Plan and say out loud what the writing will be about

Making it up

Fiction is made-up stories. A story can be about whatever the writer decides.

When writing fiction, it is important to **plan** the story first. The plan can be written down or it could be drawn on a storyboard showing each section of the story.

> **Remember**
>
> Saying your ideas out loud can help you decide if they will make a great story.

Example

This is an example of a storyboard plan:

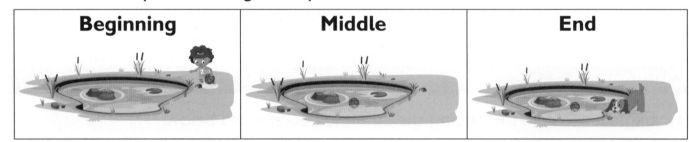

Beginning	Middle	End

Composing the story

Composition means writing the story using complete sentences in each section.

> **Tip**
>
> Ask somebody else to read your writing too in case you make any mistakes.

Example

Beginning

One day, Ben went to the park. It was a lovely day. Ben played with his new ball next to the duck pond.

Middle

Ben threw the ball too far and it landed in the pond. He was quite upset and didn't know how he would get the ball back.

End

Fred the dog saw the ball in the pond. He jumped in the water and swam. Fred brought the ball back to Ben. He was so happy that he gave Fred a biscuit.

> **Key words**
>
> - fiction
> - plan
> - composition

Challenge 1

1. Explain to an adult what happens in the beginning, middle and end of a story you know. Say who the characters are and where the story is set.

2 marks

Challenge 2

1. Draw lines to match each sentence to the part of a story you think it comes from.

| It was a dark, wet day. | Finally, they made it. What a great adventure it had been! | The children were brave but they knew their problems were not over. |

beginning　　　　　　　**middle**　　　　　　　**end**

3 marks

Challenge 3

1. Say and write three sentences to describe a setting you know. (It could be your school, or a special place you visit.) Include at least one adjective in each sentence.

_____

_____

_____

_____

_____

_____

3 marks

Total: ☐ / 8 marks

Had a go ☐　　　**Getting there** ☐　　　**Got it!** ☐

Writing non-fiction

- Write about real events for different purposes
- Use commas in lists

Getting real

Non-fiction texts provide information. They are about something **real**. The writing includes **facts** and can have different purposes. For example:

- A **report** gives the reader information about something or someone.
- A **recount** tells the reader about events in the order that they happened.
- **Instructions** tell the reader how to do something.

It is important to **plan** your writing to make sure all the main facts or steps are covered.

Example

Here is a plan for a report about badgers:

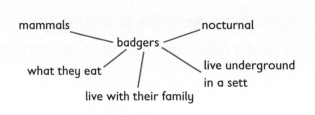

mammals — badgers — nocturnal

what they eat

live with their family

live underground in a sett

Composing your writing

Your plan may have several main points. You will then write a sentence or group of sentences for each point.

Example

Badgers are nocturnal mammals. They live with their family in an underground home called a sett. They have a diet of worms but will eat other things too such as fruit, seeds and scraps.

If you have several items to include with one point, you can use **commas** to make a list, e.g.

Badgers eat worms, fruit, seeds and food scraps.

Remember

It is important that you know what you are writing about and what the purpose of the writing is. Make sure you know the main facts.

Tip

Use commas to make lists of several items in your writing. Place the comma after each item except the next to last, which is followed by 'and'.

Key words

- non-fiction
- plan
- comma

Challenge 1

1. Write some key ideas to help you plan a piece of writing about your day.

What did you do first?

What did you do next?

_____

_____

My day

What was the best part of your day?

What is the last thing you did?

_____

_____

4 marks

Challenge 2

1. Choose one of the points in your plan above and write a sentence about it. Include an adjective in your sentence.

_____

_____

1 mark

Challenge 3

1. Write a sentence to go with each picture for instructions on growing a plant.

First, _____

_____

_____

Next, _____

_____

_____

Eventually, _____

_____

_____

3 marks

Total: [ ] /8 marks

Had a go [ ]   **Getting there** [ ]   **Got it!** [ ]

Writing poetry and description

- Write poetry
- Use description in writing

Poems

A **poem** tells a story or describes objects or feelings. Some poems **rhyme** but they do not have to.

Example

A beautiful, calm summer **sky**,
Blue with no clouds passing **by**,
A dove with feathers of brilliant **white**,
Reflecting the sun shining so **bright**.

> This poem has rhymes in pairs of lines. They are known as **couplets**.

The poem could have a different rhyming pattern:

A beautiful, calm summer **sky**,
A dove with feathers of brilliant **white**,
Flutters gently passing **by**,
Reflecting the sun shining so **bright**.

> In this poem every other line rhymes.

Remember

Use adjectives and adverbs for description.

Using description

Poems and most pieces of writing sound better when they contain description – this is often through the use of **adjectives** to describe something (e.g. beautiful, bright) and **adverbs** to describe how something is being done (e.g. gently, slowly).

Think about the description of the sky in the poem above. 'A beautiful, calm summer sky' sounds much better than 'A nice sky'. 'Flutters gently by' sounds much better than 'Flies by'.

Think about your senses and how something might look, feel, sound, smell or taste. This can help with description.

Tip

Think about how something looks, sounds, tastes, smells or feels to help you think of **adjectives** to describe it.

Key words

- poem
- rhyme
- adjective
- adverb

Challenge 1

1. Read the poem below and think of different adjectives to replace the underlined ones in each line. (They can have a different meaning.) Write them in the spaces provided.

Scary Mary had a **dirty** _____ hog,

Which lay upon an **old** _____ log.

It only ate **stinky** _____ veg,

Found beneath the garden hedge.

Challenge 2

1. Create rhyming couplets that use each pair of words. One has been done for you.

light   *When Aunty Mo turned on the light,*
sight   *She gazed upon a terrible sight.*

a) park   _____

    dark   _____

b) feet   _____

    street   _____

Challenge 3

1. Give two or three adjectives to describe each of the things below, thinking about your senses.

a) the taste of chocolate   _____

b) the sound of a drum   _____

c) the smell of a flower   _____

Total: ☐ / 8 marks

Had a go ☐   **Getting there** ☐   **Got it!** ☐

Checking writing makes sense

- Know the importance of proofreading and editing your writing

Reading your writing

Whenever you write anything, it is important to read it, both as you write and after you have finished. This is known as **proofreading**.

Editing your writing means making corrections to spellings, punctuation or grammar, and/or adding new words.

Read your writing and ask yourself:
- Do the sentences make sense?
- Is the punctuation correct?
- Can any of the words be improved?
- Are words spelled correctly?

Remember

A sentence cannot make sense if it does not have a capital letter and the correct punctuation.

Example

This part of a recount has a few mistakes:

> **their** instead of **there**

First, we visited the lions. Their were some cubs but they were asleep ← **missing full stop**

> **missing capital letter**

next, the zookeeper showed us the giraffes. They were tall. What amazing animals they are

> **wrong tense**

> **missing exclamation mark**

Finally, we go to the elephants. One elephant was very big. It splasht water at us.

> **a better phrase than very big** might be **enormous**

> **spelling mistake – should be splashed, not splasht**

Tip

Reading your writing out loud can help you spot mistakes.

Key words

- proofreading
- editing

Read the letter and then answer the questions.

Deer Lena,

thank you for inviting me to your **partie**

It sounds fun and **i** would like to come.

I will show you my photographs from **spain**.

The beach was nice and the sea was nice.

Have you ever been **their**

See you next week.

From,
Jack

Challenge 1

1. Proofread the letter above.
   Write the red words as they should appear.

   _____   _____   _____

   _____   _____   _____

   6 marks

Challenge 2

1. Some punctuation at the end of sentences is missing. Write the correct punctuation after the letter.

   2 marks

Challenge 3

1. The words in blue are a bit 'boring'. Rewrite this sentence replacing the adjective 'nice' to make the beach and sea sound more interesting.

   _____

   _____

   _____

   2 marks

Total: ____ / 10 marks

Had a go ☐   **Getting there** ☐   **Got it!** ☐

Different types of sentences

- Write different types of sentences, including statements, commands, questions and exclamations

Statements

A **statement** is a sentence that gives clear information.

Example

- The green car had shiny, black wheels.
- Miss Jones would like that car.

Commands

A **command** contains a **verb** and can be used to make requests (ask for something politely), give instructions (tell how to do something), or give orders (demand that something be done).

Example

Please do not **touch** the car. **Open** it carefully. **Get** out, now.

Questions

A **question** is used to find out information.

Example

Who owns the blue car? **What** kind of car is it?
Where did it come from? **Why** is it parked there?
When did the owner buy it? **How** much did it cost?

Exclamations

An **exclamation** starts with 'What' or 'How', contains a **verb** and ends with an exclamation mark. Exclamation sentences are used to show strong feelings.

Example

What a scary film we saw! How lovely it is to see you!

Remember

Every type of sentence must start with a capital letter and end with correct punctuation.

Remember

A verb is a 'doing', 'being' or 'having' word, e.g.
- they played
- I am
- we have

The word at the beginning of each sentence is a question word.

Each question ends with a question mark.

Key words

- statement
- command
- verb
- question
- exclamation

Challenge 1

1. Write **statement, command, question** or **exclamation** to say what type of sentence each one is.

   a) James, please pass the pencil to me. _____

   b) What an incredible machine you made! _____

   c) How far away are those mountains? _____

   d) The book I'm reading is good. _____

   4 marks

Challenge 2

1. Complete the missing questions and statements.

   Question

   a) _____

   _____

   b) What is the dog called?

   Statement

   The dog was last seen in the park.

   _____

   _____

   2 marks

Challenge 3

1. Write one example of each type of sentence.

   Statement _____

   _____

   Command _____

   _____

   Question _____

   _____

   Exclamation _____

   _____

   4 marks

   Total: ☐ / 10 marks

   Had a go ☐   **Getting there** ☐   **Got it!** ☐

Expanded noun phrases

- Use expanded noun phrases

Expanded noun phrases

An **expanded noun phrase** contains a **pronoun**, **noun**, or a word to replace the noun, and the word or words that give you more information (e.g. **adjectives**).

Example

a green monster

the yellow eyes

Here, the noun 'monster' is described using the **adjective** 'green', which gives us more information about it. The noun 'eyes' is described using the adjective 'yellow', which gives us more information.

Providing more detail makes your writing more interesting. Try to add more adjectives. You could add a **verb** to the sentence too to say what is happening. If you add more than one adjective, use **commas** to separate them.

Example

Tilly looked at **the cute, green monster**.

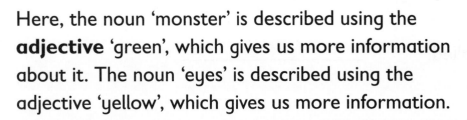

Bright, glowing, yellow eyes stared back.

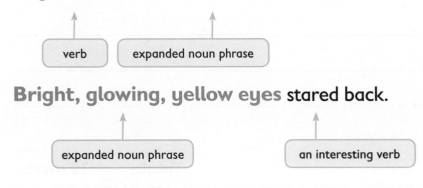

Remember

A noun is a word for a person, place or thing. The noun can sometimes be replaced by another word, e.g. he, she, it, they. These are called pronouns.

Tip

Think of interesting adjectives – try 'wonderful' instead of 'nice', or 'huge' instead of 'big'.

Key words

- expanded noun phrase
- pronoun
- noun
- adjective
- verb
- comma

Challenge 1

1. Write an adjective to complete each expanded noun phrase.

   a) The _____ snow.

   b) The _____ food.

   c) A _____ elephant.

   d) A _____ mouse.

Challenge 2

1. Add an adjective and noun to each of the sentences below to make an expanded noun phrase.

   a) Kai played with the _____ _____ .

   b) Emma ate the _____ _____ .

   c) Jess stared at the _____ _____ .

   d) Mum talked to the _____ _____ .

Challenge 3

1. Write a sentence with an expanded noun phrase for each idea.

   a) Amir and a house

   _____

   _____

   b) Henry and a burger

   _____

   _____

Total: ☐ / 16 marks

Had a go ☐   **Getting there** ☐   **Got it!** ☐

Coordination and subordination

- Use the coordination words: and, or, but
- Use the subordination words: when, if, that, because

Joining words and clauses

Words, phrases and **clauses** can often be linked using different **joining words**. These are coordination words (and, or, but) and subordination words (e.g. when, if, that, because).

Example

- **and**:
  - Belle **and** Jay like ice-cream.
  - We own a big dog **and** two little kittens.
  - The park had a playground **and** it also had a pond.
- **or**:
  - Jai doesn't like peas **or** beans.
  - The children could visit the park **or** they could go to the zoo.
- **but**:
  - Val is a good swimmer **but** a poor diver.
  - They liked the park **but** they wanted to go to the zoo.

> **Remember**
>
> Each joining word has a different meaning, so be careful which one you use.

Two clauses can be joined together using the words when, if, that or because. These are subordination words.

Example

- The children decided to go to the zoo **when** it was warmer.
- They chose the zoo **because** they liked the lions.
- The zoo was so busy **that** they could not see the lions.
- They only like the zoo **if** they can see the lions.

> **Tip**
>
> A clause is a group of words that tells us what something is doing, e.g. The children walked to town.

> **Key words**
>
> - clause
> - joining word

Challenge 1

1. Write the most appropriate joining word in each sentence.

a) The sun is shining _____ it is a warm day. **and / but**

b) You must eat breakfast _____ you will be hungry. **but / or**

c) I like the winter _____ I like the summer even more. **because / but**

d) My house has a garden _____ we have a shed. **and / if**

4 marks

Challenge 2

1. Join each pair of sentences using the most appropriate joining word. Rewrite them as one sentence.

because　　　　**if**　　　　　　**but**

a) The snow melted quickly. It was a warm day.

_____

b) The snow will melt. The sun keeps shining.

_____

c) The snow is melting. At least it is warm now.

_____

3 marks

Challenge 3

1. Write one sentence using **but** and one sentence using **if** to join ideas.

a) _____

_____

b) _____

_____

2 marks

Total: ⬜ /9 marks

| Had a go ⬜ | Getting there ⬜ | Got it! ⬜ |

Present and past tenses

- **Use the present and past tenses**

Present tense

The **present tense** is used when talking about the present, which means **now**.

The **present tense** can be changed slightly when talking about an **ongoing** action that is happening now.

Example

It **is** 1 o'clock.
I **eat** my lunch. ← Present: it is happening at this very moment.
The dog **barks**.

It **is getting** late.
I **am eating** my lunch. ← Present that is ongoing: it is happening now but is more than just a single moment – it is still going on.
The dog **is barking**.

Past tense

The **past tense** is used when talking about something that has already happened.

The **past tense** can be changed slightly when talking about an **ongoing** action that was happening in the past.

Example

It **was** 1 o'clock.
I **ate** my lunch. ← Past: it has already happened.
The dog **barked**.

It **was getting** late.
I **was eating** my lunch. ← Past that was ongoing: it was happening in the past.
The dog **was barking**.

Remember

Present tense is happening now. Past tense has already happened.

Tip

The present and past tenses always have a verb ending in -ing when talking about an ongoing action.

Key words

- present tense
- past tense

Challenge 1

1. Choose the correct word(s) to complete each sentence below.

   was writing   runs   climbing   were running   wrote   climbed

   a) This morning, the children _____ in a race.

   b) I _____ a letter when the doorbell rang.

   c) They all _____ over the wall.

Challenge 2

1. Rewrite each underlined word to show that it is an ongoing action in the **present** tense.

   a) The boat <u>sailed</u>.   The boat is _____.

   b) Luke <u>skipped</u>.   Luke is _____.

   c) They all <u>talked</u> together.   They are all _____ together.

Challenge 3

1. Complete each sentence using past or present tense verbs which show ongoing actions.

   a) Yesterday, I _____

   _____

   b) Today, we _____

   _____

   c) Yesterday, they _____

   _____

Total: ____ /9 marks

Had a go ☐   **Getting there** ☐   **Got it!** ☐

Progress test 3

1. **Circle the correct homophone to complete the sentence.**

   a) **There / They're** might be rain later.

   b) The car needs new **brakes / breaks**.

   c) I am going **too / to** the shops.

   d) He said he **knew / new** the answer.

   4 marks

2. **Write the most appropriate joining word in each sentence.**

   a) Close the window _____ the rain will come in. **but / or**

   b) I made a cake _____ it burned in the oven. **or / but**

   c) Put a coat on _____ it is cold outside. **because / or**

   d) There is a prize _____ we win the race. **and / if**

   4 marks

3. **Add an apostrophe to show possession in each sentence.**

   a) Chips and peas are Finns favourite.

   b) Four weeks until we go to Grandmas house.

   c) The cats whiskers are long.

   d) Brushes and mops are Stans tools for cleaning.

   4 marks

4. **Read each word and write how many syllables it has.**

   a) school ☐   d) yesterday ☐

   b) umbrella ☐   e) holiday ☐

   c) playground ☐   f) exclamation ☐

   6 marks

5. Read the text and then answer the questions.

Junior Park Ranger

For two years, Stephi has been a volunteer helper at her local country park. Every weekend and sometimes in school holidays, she assists the park rangers.

Many jobs need doing. One day she might be planting bulbs. On another day she could be cleaning signs or clearing paths.

Stephi's favourite job is the wildlife survey. Each month, she checks different things. In the meadow, she counts rabbits. In the woodland, she records types of birds. She likes counting the ducks and geese on the lake.

When she grows up, Stephi would like to be a park ranger. She likes the outdoors and wildlife, and she likes helping.

a) How long has Stephi been a volunteer helper? _____

b) What does the word 'assists' mean? _____

c) In the third paragraph, which word shows that she makes a note of what birds are in the woodland? _____

d) Why do you think this text is called 'Junior Park Ranger'?

_____

e) The last sentence reads, 'She likes the outdoors and wildlife, and she likes helping.' Rewrite this sentence replacing both instances of the word 'likes' with more interesting words.

_____

_____

5 marks

6. **Write statement, command, question or exclamation to say what type of sentence each one is. Then add the correct punctuation.**

   a) How incredibly beautiful it is___   _____

   b) What type of cat is that ___   _____

   c) Stand up immediately ___   _____

   d) Danny has got a pet rabbit ___   _____

8 marks

7. **Circle the correct homophone for each sentence.**

   a) We will get **there / their** this evening.

   b) Nobody could **see / sea** where they were hiding.

   c) Can you **here / hear** the sound of thunder?

   d) They left the light on at **night / knight**.

   e) The leaves had all fallen, leaving the tree **bare / bear**.

   f) The flowers were **blew / blue**, red and yellow.

6 marks

8. **Add two adjectives to create an expanded noun phrase from each noun.**

   flowers   _____

   snow   _____

   car   _____

3 marks

9. **Write a sentence including a verb and an expanded noun phrase for each idea.**

   a) Dad and a pet rabbit

   _____

   b) Grace and a school bag

   _____

2 marks

10. **Read the poem and then answer the questions.**

   Hometime

   Children waiting for the bell
   To give them the signal
   That it's time to go.

   Adults waiting at the gate
   For children to run
   Joyfully into their arms.

   a) What is the signal that tells the children it is time to go?

   _____

   b) Who are the adults waiting for? _____

   c) What does the word 'joyfully' mean? _____

   d) Which word in the poem is a contraction? _____

4 marks

Total: [ ] /46 marks

Recognising fractions

- Recognise, name, and write fractions
- Recognise equivalence

Features of a fraction

A **fraction** is part of a whole object, group of objects or number. A fraction is made up of the **numerator** (at the top) and the **denominator** (at the bottom).

A **unit fraction** (such as $\frac{1}{2}$) has a numerator of 1.

Recognising simple fractions

To recognise a **half**, you must be able to spot that the object or number has been divided into **two equal parts**. One of these parts is one half, written as $\frac{1}{2}$.

One quarter of an object or number means it has been divided into **four equal parts**. One of these parts is one quarter, written as $\frac{1}{4}$.

Three quarters of an object or number means it has been divided into **four equal parts.** Three of those parts make three quarters, written as $\frac{3}{4}$.

One third of an object or number means it has been divided into **three equal parts**. One of these parts is one third, written as $\frac{1}{3}$.

Numerator: how many parts of the whole you have.

$$\frac{1}{2}$$

Denominator: how many equal parts there are in the whole.

Remember

$\frac{1}{1}$ means a whole.

$\frac{2}{4}$ is equal to $\frac{1}{2}$

Tip

Look for lines of symmetry between shapes, objects, and arrays. This will help you to spot the different fractions.

Key words

- fraction
- numerator
- denominator
- unit fraction
- half

Challenge 1

1. Tick the shape that has one quarter coloured in.

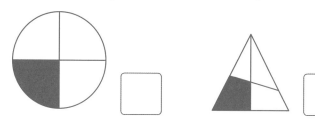

2. Tick the shape that has been divided into thirds.

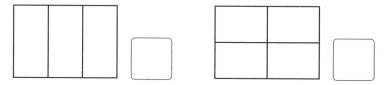

2 marks

Challenge 2

1. Tick the picture in which $\frac{1}{4}$ of the beads are next to the jar.

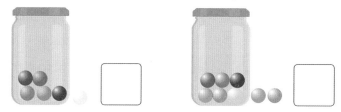

2. Tick the pizza that has had $\frac{1}{3}$ eaten.

2 marks

Challenge 3

1. Circle the number sentence that shows quarters.

   2 + 2 + 2 + 2   5 + 5 + 5 + 5 + 5

2. Circle the number sentence that shows thirds.

   2 + 2 + 2 + 2   1 + 1 + 1

3. Circle the number sentence that shows halves.

   10 + 10   2 + 2 + 2 + 2

3 marks

Total: [ ] /7 marks

Had a go [ ]   Getting there [ ]   Got it! [ ]

Finding fractions

- Recognise and find fractions
- Recognise equivalence

Fractions for dividing equally

To find a certain **fraction**, a shape, number or set of objects must be shared or grouped equally into the **denominator**. Then consider how many parts from the **numerator** you need.

Finding a half, quarters and a third

To find half, you must be able to **divide** the shape, or share/group the objects/amounts, into **two equal parts**. This is ÷ **2**. This is also 1 in every 2.

6 out of 12 oranges have been circled.

$$\frac{6}{12} = \frac{1}{2}$$

To find one quarter, you must be able to divide the shape, or share/group the objects/amounts, into **four equal parts**. This is ÷ **4**. This is also 1 in every 4.

 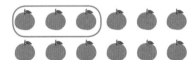

3 out of 12 oranges have been circled.

$$\frac{3}{12} = \frac{1}{4}$$

To find three quarters, you must be able to divide the shape, or share/group the objects/amounts, into **four equal parts**. Three of these parts make $\frac{3}{4}$. This is ÷ **4** then **x 3**. This is also 3 in every 4.

9 out of 12 oranges have been circled.

$$\frac{9}{12} = \frac{3}{4}$$

To find one third you must be able to divide the shape, or share/group the objects/amounts into **three equal parts**. This is ÷ **3**. This is also 1 in every 3.

 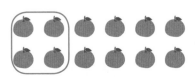

4 out of 12 oranges have been circled.

$$\frac{4}{12} = \frac{1}{3}$$

Challenge 1

1. Shade $\frac{1}{4}$ of the shapes.

   a) 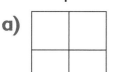   b)

2. Shade $\frac{1}{3}$ of the shapes.

   a)    b)

Challenge 2

1. Draw a circle around $\frac{1}{4}$ of the spots. Complete the number sentence to show the quarter.

$$\boxed{} \div 4 = \boxed{}$$

2. Draw a circle around $\frac{1}{3}$ of the spots. Complete the number sentence to show the third.

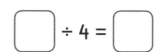

$$\boxed{} \div 3 = \boxed{}$$

3. Draw a circle around $\frac{3}{4}$ of the spots. Complete the number sentence to show three quarters.

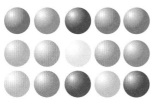

$$\boxed{} \div 4 = \text{(then x 3)} = \boxed{}$$

Challenge 3

1. Complete the table. The first row has been done for you. (It might help you to draw an array and use grouping to find the fractions.)

Number	$\frac{1}{2}$	$\frac{1}{4}$	$\frac{1}{3}$	$\frac{3}{4}$
8	4	2		6
12				
16				
18				
24				

Total: [ ] /20 marks

Had a go [ ]   **Getting there** [ ]   **Got it!** [ ]

Estimating and measuring

- Estimate and measure length and height, mass and capacity
- Compare and order measures using >, < and =

What are units of measure?

Standard units of measure are amounts used for measuring and recording. Measurements can be compared and ordered using **>** (more than), **<** (less than) and **=** (equals). It is sometimes helpful to make **estimates**. An estimate is a good guess based on what you know and what you can see in front of you.

Length, height, mass and capacity

The standard units used to measure **length** and **height** are centimetres (cm) and metres (m). There are 100 cm in 1 m.

Example

> The length of the pencil is 12 cm.

The standard units used to measure **mass**, or **weight**, are grams (g) and kilograms (kg). There are 1,000 g in 1 kg.

Example

 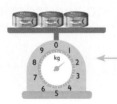

> The weight of the cheese is 1 kg. The weight of the tuna is 1.5 or $1\frac{1}{2}$ kg. So, cheese < tuna.

The standard units used to measure **capacity** are millilitres (ml) and litres (*l*). Capacity is the amount of liquid a container can hold. There are 1,000 ml in 1 *l*.

Example

> The capacity of the first jug is 1 *l* (1,000 ml) and is full. The capacity of the second jug is still 1 *l* (1,000 ml) but this time it is only half full (500 ml). So jug 1 > jug 2.

Remember

Length and height can be described as being long or short. Mass can be described as being heavy or light.

Tip

Kilo means 1,000 (one thousand). This should help you remember that 1 kilogram (kg) is 1,000 grams and 1 kilometre (km) is 1,000 metres (m).

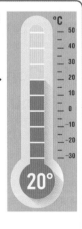

Temperature can also be measured. A thermometer is used to measure temperature. Here, the temperature is showing 20°C.

Key words

- estimate
- length/height
- mass/weight
- capacity

Challenge 1

1. Write the letters in the boxes to put the pencils in order from shortest to longest.

☐ ☐ ☐ ☐ ☐

Shortest   **Longest**

A ▭ 3 cm
B ▭ 9 cm
C ▭ 6 cm
D ▭ 1 cm
E ▭ 20 cm

2. Estimate the length of the pencil. Do not use a ruler. Write the answer in the box.

☐ cm

☐ 6 marks

Challenge 2

1. Look at the measurements and write **<** , **>** or **=** in each box.

1 kg

900 kg

200 g

a) 20 g ☐

b) ☐ 2,000 g

c) ☐ 900 kg

☐ 3 marks

Challenge 3

1. a) How much water is in the jug? Write the answer in the box.

☐ litres

5 Ltr
4 Ltr
3 Ltr
2 Ltr
1 Ltr
0

b) How much is this in ml? _____ ml

☐ 2 marks

Total: ☐ / 11 marks

Had a go ☐   **Getting there** ☐   **Got it!** ☐

Money

- Recognise and use symbols for pounds (£) and pence (p)
- Combine amounts to make a particular value
- Find different combinations of coins that equal the same amounts of money

Units of money

In the UK, the standard units of money or **currency** are **pounds (£)** and **pence (p)**.

Pounds can be coins or notes depending on their value. These are the notes and the coins:

When combining an amount of money, you should total pounds and pence separately.

Example

    This amount is **£6** and **25p**.

Coins and notes can be used in different combinations to make the same amount.

Example

Look at the coins. Each of the three groups total 50p.

What is change?

If you buy something at a shop and pay with too much money, you will be given some money or 'change' back.

Example

Zak buys a pencil costing 55p. He gives the shopkeeper £1. She gives Zak 45p change. This is a subtraction:

£1 (Zak's money) **– 55p** (cost of the pencil) **= 45p** (change)

Remember

Counting in 2ps, 5ps and 10ps is the same as the 2, 5 and 10 times tables.

Tip

Think of £10 as being a Dienes stick. Think of £1 as being a Dienes cube.

Key word

- currency

Challenge 1

PS 1. a) Count the money and write the total.

⬡P

b) Count the money and write the total.

£ ⬡ and ⬡ P

Challenge 2

1. Complete the table. Draw or write three different combinations of coins to make 80p.

Combination 1	
Combination 2	
Combination 3	

2. Complete the table.

Pounds	Pence	Total		
4	35	£	and	p
6		£	and 74	p
	41	£ 9	and	p

Challenge 3

1. Complete the bar model. The three boxes at the bottom are equal shares of the amount in the top box.

£30

⬜ ⬜ ⬜

2. Fill in the gaps to make the statement correct.

£10 + £5 + 50p + 10p = £ ⬜ and ⬜ p

Total: ⬜ / 13 marks

Had a go ⬜   **Getting there** ⬜   **Got it!** ⬜

Telling the time and periods of time

- Compare and sequence intervals of time
- Tell the time to five minutes
- Know the number of minutes in an hour and the number of hours in a day

Time

Time is the word that we use to measure how long something takes to do, or how long something lasts.

Small measures of time	Large measures of time
60 seconds = 1 minute	7 days = 1 week
30 minutes = $\frac{1}{2}$ an hour	2 weeks = 1 fortnight
60 minutes = 1 hour	(approximately) 4 weeks = 1 month
24 hours = 1 day	52 weeks = 1 year

Analogue clocks: hour and minutes

Example

This **analogue clock** is showing 4 o'clock.

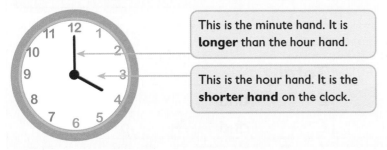

This is the minute hand. It is **longer** than the hour hand.

This is the hour hand. It is the **shorter hand** on the clock.

When the minute hand is pointing to 12, it is showing a full hour. We call this time **o'clock**.

The numbers on the clock mean **hours** for the hour hand. They also mean **every 5 minutes** for the minute hand. (This is like the 5 times table.)

These are all on the **to** side of the clock (**to the hour**). These are the red numbers on the clock above.

When the minute hand is at 7, it means **25 minutes to**; 8 means **20 to**; 9 means **quarter to** (15 minutes to); 10 means **10 to** and 11 means **5 to**.

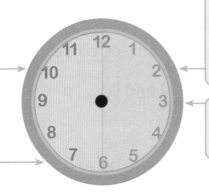

When the minute hand is at 1, it means **5 minutes past**; at 2 means **10 past**; at 3 means **quarter past** (15 minutes past); at 4 means **20 past**; at 5 means **25 past** and at 6 means **half past** (30 minutes past).

These are all on the **past** side of the clock (**past the hour**). These are the blue numbers on the clock above.

> **Remember**
>
> The minute hand takes half an hour to move halfway around the clock and one hour to go all the way around.

> **Tip**
>
> Think of a clock like a pizza or cake: there are quarters worth 15 minutes and halves worth 30 minutes.

> **Key word**
>
> - analogue clock

Challenge 1

1. Read the time on the clocks. Write the answer on the line in words.

a)

_____

b)

_____

2 marks

Challenge 2

1. Draw the hands on the clocks to show the time.

a) 20 past 1

b) 5 past 4

c) 10 to 6

d) 25 to 3

4 marks

Challenge 3

1. Look at the clocks. Follow the instruction for each. Write the answer on the line.

a)    Write the time 1 hour later.

_____

b)    Write the time 40 minutes earlier.

_____

2 marks

Total: [ ] /8 marks

Had a go [ ]   Getting there [ ]   Got it! [ ]

2-D shapes

- Identify and describe the properties of 2-D shapes, including the number of sides and line symmetry in a vertical line
- Compare and sort common 2-D shapes

What does 2-D mean?

2-D means 2 dimensional; 2-D shapes have two dimensions.

Here are some common 2-D shapes:

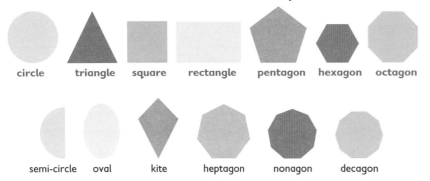

circle   triangle   square   rectangle   pentagon   hexagon   octagon

semi-circle   oval   kite   heptagon   nonagon   decagon

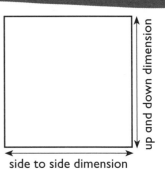

side to side dimension

up and down dimension

Symmetry of 2-D shapes

Symmetry means that if a line is drawn through the middle of a shape, both sides are the same.

Example

This square is divided into two equal parts by a **line of symmetry**.

Comparing properties

Some of the more common 2-D shapes have been placed in this table according to their properties. Properties include the number of sides, the lengths of sides and the corners.

Fewer than 3 sides and 0 corners	3 sides and 3 corners	4 sides and 4 corners	More than 4 sides and 4 corners
Circle Oval	Triangle	Square Rectangle Kite	Pentagon Hexagon Octagon Heptagon Decagon Nonagon

> ### Remember
>
> Many 2-D shapes have more than one line of symmetry.

> ### Tip
>
> Draw and cut out some 2-D shapes and then fold them in half. See which shapes are symmetrical.

> ### Key words
>
> - 2-D shapes
> - circle
> - triangle
> - square
> - rectangle
> - pentagon
> - hexagon
> - octagon
> - symmetry

Challenge 1

1. Tick the shapes that have a line of symmetry drawn on.

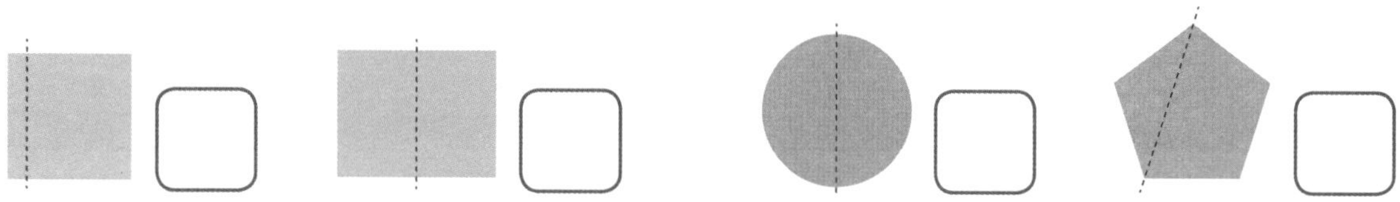

Challenge 2

1. For each of the shapes, fill in the boxes to show what properties it has.

Number of sides: ☐ Number of corners: ☐

Number of sides: ☐ Number of corners: ☐

Number of sides: ☐ Number of corners: ☐

Number of sides: ☐ Number of corners: ☐

Challenge 3

1. Write the names of the shapes in the correct place on the Venn diagram.

oval   circle   semi-circle   square   triangle   pentagon   octagon

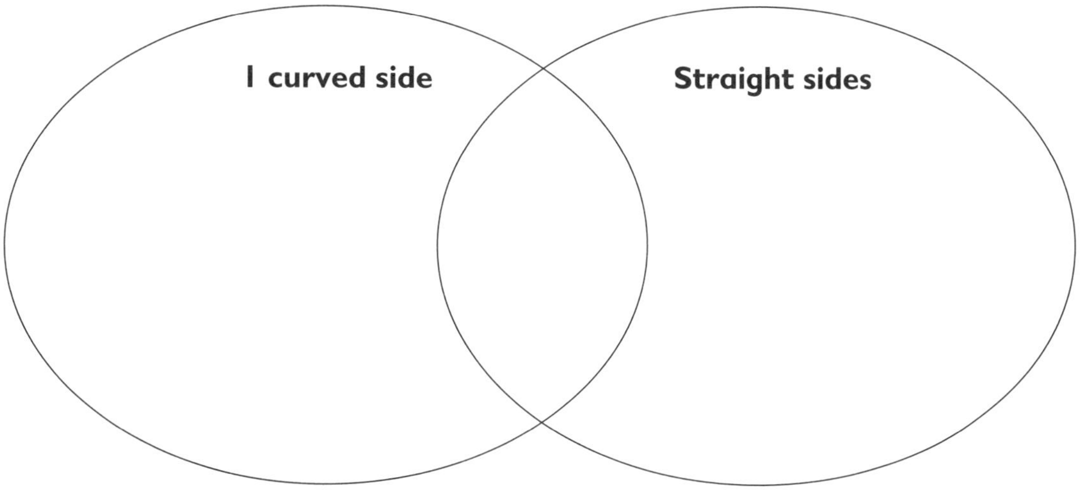

I curved side

Straight sides

Total: ☐ / 16 marks

Had a go ☐   **Getting there** ☐   **Got it!** ☐

3-D shapes

- Identify and describe the properties of 3-D shapes
- Identify 2-D shapes on the surfaces of 3-D shapes
- Compare and sort common 3-D shapes and everyday objects

What does 3-D mean?

3-D means 3 dimensional; **3-D shapes** have three dimensions.

3-D shapes are not flat; they are solid and have a depth.

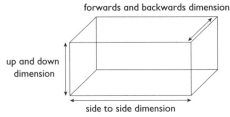

forwards and backwards dimension

up and down dimension

side to side dimension

Here are some common 3-D shapes:

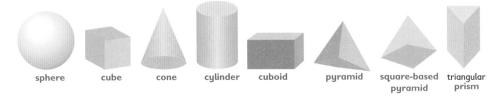

sphere   cube   cone   cylinder   cuboid   pyramid   square-based pyramid   triangular prism

> **Remember**
>
> The structure of 3-D shapes, when drawn on paper, may show missing edges with dashed lines. These represent the parts of the 3-D shape that you can't see.

Comparing properties

The properties of 3-D shapes are the **faces**, **edges** and the **vertices**.

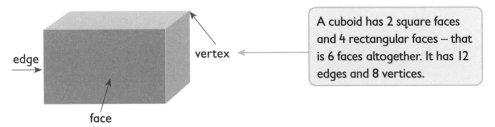

edge

vertex

face

> A cuboid has 2 square faces and 4 rectangular faces – that is 6 faces altogether. It has 12 edges and 8 vertices.

Some 3-D shapes are more common than others. These shapes have been placed in this table according to their properties.

Fewer than 3 faces	3 faces	4 faces	More than 4 faces
Sphere	Cylinder	Pyramid	Cube
Cone			Cuboid
			Square-based pyramid
			Prism

> **Key words**
>
> - 3-D shapes
> - sphere
> - cube
> - cone
> - cylinder
> - cuboid
> - pyramid/square-based pyramid
> - prism
> - face
> - vertices

Challenge 1

1. Complete the table.

Shape	Name	Faces	Edges	Vertices
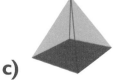				

12 marks

Challenge 2

PS 1. Solve the riddle! What shape is it?

I have 2 flat circular faces.

I have 1 curved face.

What am I?

I am a _____

1 mark

Challenge 3

1. Write down the 2-D shapes that are faces on the 3-D shapes. Some shapes have more than one face.

a) _____ _____

b) _____ _____

c) _____ _____

6 marks

Total: ☐ /19 marks

Had a go ☐	Getting there ☐	Got it! ☐

Positioning and sequencing

- Order and arrange combinations of mathematical objects in patterns and sequences

Position

Position simply means where something is.

Example

You could describe the positions of these shapes as:

On the far left is a blue square. Second from the left is a red triangle. In the middle is a green circle. Second from the right is a yellow rectangle. On the far right is a purple pentagon.

Patterns and sequences

A **pattern** or sequence is when the order of something is **repeated**.

Example

Look at the sequence of triangles. Can you see a repeating pattern?

Firstly, all the shapes are triangles. The first two triangles are red, then there is one blue triangle. So, the sequence is 2 red triangles and 1 blue triangle.

For more complicated sequences, it is best to 'chunk' the sequence into smaller parts by finding groups.

Example

Find a chunk of the sequence. For example, two blue squares, a red triangle, a green circle and a yellow triangle.

Challenge 1

1. Look at the sequence.

   a) Which shape is first? _____

   b) Which shape is third? _____

   c) Which shape is in the middle? _____

   d) Which shape is fourth? _____

   e) Which shape is next to last? _____

2. Draw the next three shapes in the sequence.

   6 marks

Challenge 2

1. Draw a repeating sequence of your own in the grid below. The repeating sequence must have no more than 4 shapes and can be any colour you want. Include the following shapes: circle, square, triangle.

   3 marks

Challenge 3

1. Draw the next shape in the sequence.

2. Write a sentence to show what the next three shapes would be (after the one you have drawn).

   _____

   2 marks

   Total: [   ] / 11 marks

   Had a go [ ]   **Getting there** [ ]   **Got it!** [ ]

Position, direction, movement and turn

- Describe position, direction and movement
- Understand right-angles for quarter, half and three-quarter turns
- Understand the terms clockwise and anti-clockwise

Describing position

Positional language is used to describe where someone or something is. In this grid, the turtle is in the **middle** or the **centre**.

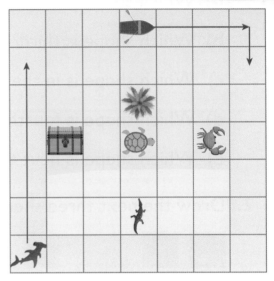

Movement and direction

Movement or **motion** means someone or something is travelling. **Direction** describes if the movement is **up**, **down**, **forwards**, **backwards**, **left** or **right**. Direction can also be used to say which way someone or something is **facing**.

Example

In the grid above: *The shark moves up 5 squares. The boat moves to the right 3 squares and down 1 square.*

Turning

Turns can be measured using these descriptions:

- Clockwise or anti-clockwise
- A **full turn** all the way round is like a whole turn. If the turtle turns around fully, it will still face the crab.
- A **half-turn** is turning to face the opposite way. If the turtle makes a half-turn, it will face the treasure chest.
- A **quarter turn** is also called a **right-angle turn**. If the turtle turns a quarter turn clockwise, it will face the crocodile. If it turns a quarter turn anti-clockwise, it will face the palm tree.
- A **three-quarter turn** – if the turtle turns a three-quarter turn clockwise (to the right), it will face the palm tree. If it turns a three-quarter turn anti-clockwise, it will face the crocodile.

> **Remember**
>
> The hands of a clock turn 'clockwise'. If the hands turned the other way, this would be 'anti-clockwise'.

> **Tip**
>
> The numbers 12, 3, 6 and 9 from a clock show the quarter turns.

> **Key words**
>
> - position
> - clockwise
> - anti-clockwise
> - turn

Use this picture to complete all the questions.

Key

🚤 Boat
🦈 Shark
🐢 Turtle
🐊 Crocodile
🦀 Crab
🧰 Treasure chest
🌴 Palm tree

Challenge 1

1. a) What is the turtle facing? _____ .

   b) The turtle needs to move ⬚ squares to reach the crocodile.

   c) The shark needs to move ⬚ squares to reach the boat.

   ⬚ 3 marks

Challenge 2

1. Complete the sentences. Fill in the missing word.

   a) The turtle turns a full turn. It is facing the _____ .

   b) The turtle turns a half-turn. It is facing the _____ .

   c) The turtle turns a right-angle turn anti-clockwise. It is facing the

   _____ .

   ⬚ 3 marks

Challenge 3

1. Follow the instructions below. Draw the turtle in the new square.

   The turtle turns three quarters of a turn clockwise.
   Then the turtle moves forward two squares.
   The turtle turns one quarter of a turn anti-clockwise.
   Then the turtle moves forward two squares.

   ⬚ 1 mark

   Total: ⬚ /7 marks

Had a go ⬚   Getting there ⬚   Got it! ⬚

Tally charts and pictograms

- Interpret simple tally charts and pictograms
- Ask and answer questions by counting the objects in each category and sorting the categories by quantity
- Ask and answer questions about totalling and comparing categorical data

What is data?

Data is information. You can share data by displaying it in a **chart** or **graph**. Often, data is recorded to find out how popular something is.

Tally charts

A **tally chart** is used to collect data. It counts in **lots of five**. A vertical line represents one, then 5 is shown by drawing a line through the four vertical lines.

Example

This tally chart shows the pets that children have at home in Year 2.

Pets	Tally
Dog	ⅢⅠ ⅢⅠ
Cat	ⅢⅠ
Rabbit	ⅢⅠ |||
Guinea pig	|||

> The category with the biggest tally (10) shows the most popular pet – a dog.

> The category with the smallest tally (3) shows the least popular pet – a guinea pig.

Pictograms

A **pictogram** shows information using pictures. It can take the data of a tally chart and show it in picture form.

Example

This pictogram matches the tally chart above. It is a different way of showing the same information.

Dog	👤👤👤👤👤👤👤👤👤👤
Cat	👤👤👤👤👤
Rabbit	👤👤👤👤👤👤👤👤
Guinea pig	👤👤👤

👤 = 1 pet

> 10 children have a dog, 5 children have a cat, 8 children have a rabbit and 3 children have a guinea pig.

Challenge 1

1. Year 2 is trying to find out what the most popular fruit is amongst the children in the class. Each child votes for their favourite fruit.
Use this picture to gather the data and complete the tally chart.

Favourite fruit	Tally
Apple	
Banana	
Pear	
Orange	
Strawberry	

5 marks

Challenge 2

1. Complete this pictogram to show the data collected from Challenge 1.
Use the key to complete the pictogram to show the number of children who chose that fruit as their favourite.

Key

⚲ = 1 child

5 marks

Challenge 3

1. Answer the questions using the data in Challenge 1 and 2.

   a) Which was the most popular fruit? _____

   b) Which was the least popular fruit? _____

   c) How many children chose banana? _____

   d) How many more children chose orange than strawberry? _____

   e) How many children are there in Year 2? _____

5 marks

Total: ____ / 15 marks

Had a go ☐   **Getting there** ☐   **Got it!** ☐

Block graphs

- Interpret and construct simple block graphs and tables
- Ask and answer questions about the data

Block graphs

Block graphs show **data** using a number scale. They are better at showing larger amounts.

Data can be recorded in a tally chart or table and then used to create a block graph.

Example

Here is a tally chart showing the different colour snail shells that were seen one morning at the seaside.
The same information can also be shown in a table.

Tally chart

Colour of snail shell	Tally
Grey	卌 卌 卌 卌
White	卌 卌 卌
Orange	卌 卌
Brown	卌 卌 卌 卌 卌 卌
Green	卌

Table

Colour of snail shell	Total
Grey	20
White	15
Orange	10
Brown	30
Green	5

This information can be put in a block graph with a **number scale** at the side that goes up in groups of 5. So, you can show how many snails were found by counting in 5s.

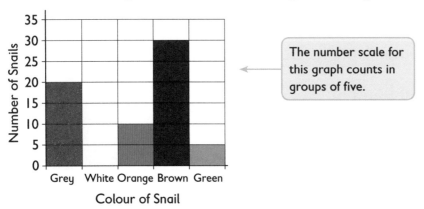

The number scale for this graph counts in groups of five.

You can use the information in the graph to ask and answer questions about what it shows.

Challenge 1

1. The children in Year 2 are trying to find out what the most popular colour is amongst the children in school. Each child votes for their favourite colour.
   Use the picture to gather the data needed and complete the tally chart.

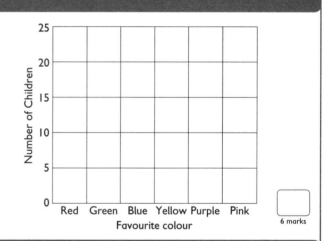

Favourite colour	Tally
Red	
Green	
Blue	
Yellow	
Purple	
Pink	

Key: One coloured square = 5 children

6 marks

Challenge 2

1. Complete the block graph to show the data collected in Challenge 1. Shade in the boxes in the graph to show the number of children who chose that colour as their favourite. Remember to check the scale!

Number of Children

25
20
15
10
5
0

Red Green Blue Yellow Purple Pink

Favourite colour

6 marks

Challenge 3

1. Answer the questions using the data in Challenges 1 and 2.

   a) Which was the most popular colour? _____

   b) How many children chose the most popular colour? _____

   c) Which was the least popular colour? _____

   d) How many children chose pink? _____

   e) How many children are there in total? _____

   5 marks

   Total: ____ / 17 marks

Had a go ☐   **Getting there** ☐   **Got it!** ☐

Progress test 4

1. Colour $\frac{3}{4}$ of this shape.

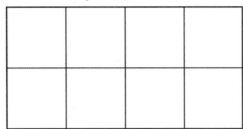

1 mark

2. James has 18 marbles. He wants to share them between his friends. They get $\frac{1}{3}$ each. Circle $\frac{1}{3}$ of the marbles.

1 mark

3. There is 250 g of sugar on the scale. Draw the arrow on the scale to show where it would be pointing.

1 mark

4. Use < , > or = to make the statements correct.

1 kg ☐ 500 g   2,000 g ☐ 2 kg   400 g ☐ 4,000 g

3 marks

5. Draw hands on the clocks to show the time.

a) 5 past 6

b) Half past 10

2 marks

6. Look at the grid showing a turtle and a parrot.

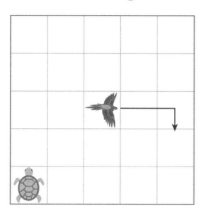

a) The turtle moves forwards 3 squares and makes a quarter turn clockwise, then moves forwards another 3 squares.

Draw an **X** on the grid to show where the turtle has moved to.

b) Complete the sentences to show how the parrot moves as shown on the grid. Use the words and numbers below to help.

I   quarter   3   clockwise   6   full   2   anti-clockwise

The parrot moves forward (right) ⬜ squares and turns a

_____ turn _____.

⬜ 4 marks

7. Name the 3-D shape, then write how many faces, edges and vertices there are.

Name of shape _____

Number of faces ⬜

Number of edges ⬜

Number of vertices ⬜

⬜ 4 marks

8. Fill in the answers.

$\frac{1}{4}$ of 16 = ⬜ $\frac{1}{3}$ of 12 = ⬜ $\frac{2}{4}$ of 20 = ⬜ $\frac{3}{4}$ of 28 = ⬜

⬜ 4 marks

9. How tall is Eva?

150cm
100cm
50cm
0cm

_____

1 mark

10. Read the time on the clocks. Write the answers in words.

a)

b)

a) _____

b) _____

2 marks

11. What fraction of the shape is shaded?

1 mark

12. Solve the riddle! What shape is it? Tick the correct answer.

I have 5 faces.
I have 2 triangular faces.
I have 6 vertices.

Pyramid ☐   Triangular prism ☐   Cuboid ☐   Sphere ☐

1 mark

13. Draw hands on the clocks to show these times:

a) 12 o'clock

b) Quarter past 10

2 marks

14. Draw the next three shapes in the sequence.

3 marks

102

15. Children in Year 2 recorded how many vehicles drove past their school in half an hour. They recorded the data in a table.

Vehicle	Tally	Total
Car	卌 卌	
Lorry		9
Bus	卌 III	
Motorbike		4
Van	III	
Bicycle		I

6 marks

a) Complete the table.

b) Which vehicle drove past the school the most? _____

c) How many more lorries drove past the school than vans?

d) Which 2 vehicles combined to total 10? _____

e) Write a question you could ask about the data.

_____

4 marks

16. Name the 2-D shape, then say how many sides and how many corners there are.

Name of shape _____

Number of sides

Number of corners

3 marks

17. Use a ruler to draw a line of symmetry on the shape below.

1 mark

Total: _____ /44 marks

103

English mixed questions

1. **Write the correct word in the spaces given to complete the sentences.**

   know   **gnaw**   **knocked**   **written**

   a) They _____ on the door.

   b) I have _____ a letter to you.

   c) Why don't I _____ where it is?

   d) The dog likes to _____ his bone.

   4 marks

2. **Read the text and then answer the questions.**

   ### The Drama Club

   Alice and Lucas are in the school drama club. Each term they rehearse and perform a different show. Their parents and friends are invited to watch.

   Some shows have singing and dancing in them. Alice loves singing but she finds the dancing very tricky. Lucas has been asked to play his guitar in a show but is nervous about this.

   The children in the club take it in turns to do other jobs such as making costumes and changing scenery. Lots of hard work goes into each production.

   a) What does the word 'rehearse' mean? _____

   b) Apart from performing, what other jobs are there to do in drama club?

   _____   _____

   c) Why do you think Lucas is nervous about playing his guitar in a show?

   _____

   4 marks

3. **Read the sentences below. At the end of each line, correctly write the contraction of the underlined words.**

   a) <u>You are</u> coming to my house for tea. _____

   b) We <u>could not</u> find the ball. _____

   c) <u>I will</u> go to school tomorrow. _____

   d) There <u>are not</u> enough chips to share. _____

   e) <u>She is</u> going to be late. _____ ☐

   5 marks

4. **Complete the passage below. Use the words given and add the correct ending to each.**

   copy   **reply**   **try**   **carry**   **fly**

   Ella knocked on the door but nobody r_____. They had

   t _____ every house now and were so tired. They had c _____

   their packs all day. They wished they were c _____ the other

   group now and f _____ home tonight. ☐

   5 marks

5. **Complete each sentence with the correct form of the verb to show the action is ongoing in the present tense.**

   a) Zayn runs home.   Zayn _____ _____ home.

   b) Adam eats the cake.   Adam _____ _____ the cake.

   c) We pour the water.   We _____ _____ the water.

   d) They draw pictures.   They _____ _____ pictures. ☐

   4 marks

6. **Read each of the words below and then write the root word.**

   a) hiking _____

   b) shiny _____

   c) babies _____

   d) careless _____

   e) happier _____

   f) plentiful _____

6 marks

7. **Rewrite each pair of sentences as one sentence using an appropriate joining word.**

   a) You will be dizzy. You keep spinning round.

   _____

   b) We are going home now. It is getting dark.

   _____

   c) The car was old. At least it still worked.

   _____

3 marks

8. **Write a word with a similar meaning to each underlined word.**

   a) Suki <u>liked</u> the film. _____

   b) The house was <u>dirty</u>. _____

   c) James <u>shouted</u> for help. _____

3 marks

9. **Say and write three sentences to describe your house. Remember to use adjectives.**

_____

_____

_____

3 marks

10. **Write one example of each type of sentence.**

Statement _____

Command _____

Question _____

Exclamation _____

4 marks

11. **Write a sentence to go with each picture giving instructions for brushing teeth.**

a) First, _____

_____

_____

b) Next, _____

_____

_____

2 marks

12. **Read the text, then answer the questions.**

> For a long time, Gaby had wanted to be in a race. Now she had a new wheelchair she would be able to. First, she had to make her arms stronger. **Every day, she trained hard** at the gym. It was tough but **she never gave up.**

a) What do the highlighted words infer about Gaby? Tick one.

She likes her wheelchair. ☐

She is scared. ☐

She is determined. ☐

b) What do you predict will happen?

_____ ☐

2 marks

13. **Complete the expanded noun phrases by adding an adjective and a noun.**

a) The cat chased the _____ _____ .

b) George looked at the _____ _____ .

c) Snow fell on the _____ _____ .

d) Olivia walked past the _____ _____ . ☐

8 marks

14. **Read the sentences below. Write each sentence again to include an adverb to show how the action happened.**

a) The tortoise walked _____ along the road.

_____

b) The hare ran _____ ahead of the tortoise.

_____

15. **Find the word that needs an apostrophe in each of the sentences below. Rewrite the word with the apostrophe in the correct place.**

a) Devon lives on his mums boat. _____

b) I was looking for Toms hat. _____

c) The girl played with the boys game. _____

d) I'm going to my best friends birthday party. _____

16. **Read the poem and then answer the questions.**

The sunlight shines on the clear blue sea,
Shimmering patterns all around me.
Out of the water rise the smooth grey humps
And we watch, fascinated, as the dolphins jump.

The waves lap the sides of the bright, white boat
That reflects in the water like a mirror that's afloat.
All too soon we're heading back to shore,
And I can't believe I've never been here before!

a) Which word in the poem rhymes with 'me'? _____

b) Which three words describe the dolphins?

_____   _____   _____

c) Which word in the poem means the same as 'leap'? _____

d) Which two adjectives describe the boat?

_____   _____

Total: ☐ /66 marks

Maths mixed questions

1. Write the missing numbers in this sequence.

   0   ☐   6   9   ☐

   2 marks

PS 2. James rolls two dice and adds the numbers together.

   He rolls a third dice. His total score is now **14**.
   What was the number on the **third dice**?

   ☐

   1 mark

3. Complete these division calculations from the 2 times table.

   a) 20   ÷   2   =   ☐

   b) ☐   ÷   2   =   9

   2 marks

4. What fraction of these shapes has been shaded?

   a) 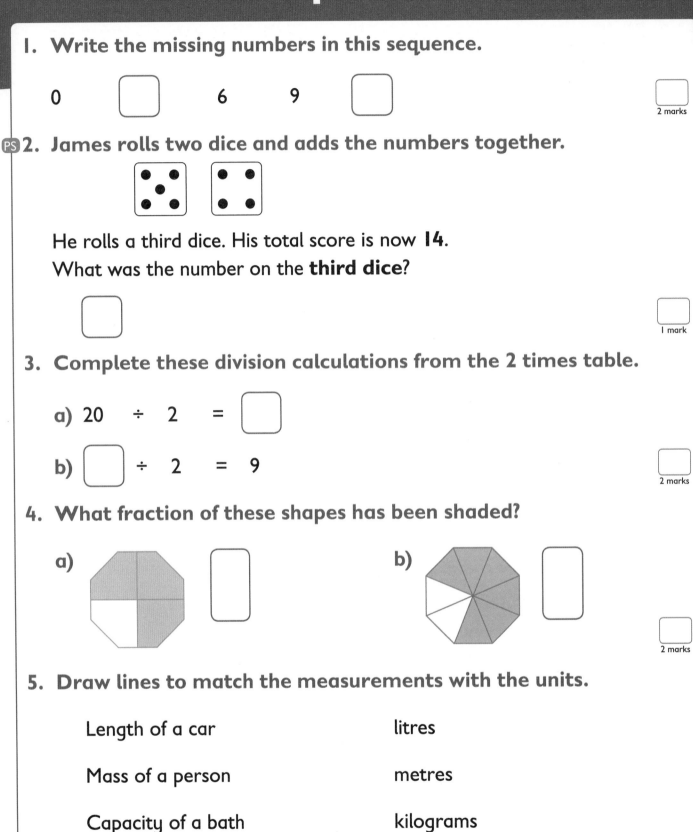 ☐   b) ☐

   2 marks

5. Draw lines to match the measurements with the units.

Length of a car	litres
Mass of a person	metres
Capacity of a bath	kilograms
Length of a pen	centimetres

   4 marks

6. Write each word in the correct space to describe the properties of a square-based pyramid.

faces   **edges**   **vertices**

A square-based pyramid has:

8 _____   5 _____   5 _____

PS 7. Below is a tally chart showing children's favourite outdoor toys.

Favourite toy	Tally
Roller skates	IIII
Scooter	IIII IIII IIII
Bike	IIII IIII IIII II
Skateboard	I
Tricycle	

a) 6 children chose tricycle. Complete the tally chart to show this.

b) Which toy was 3 times more popular than roller skates?

_____

c) Put the outdoor toys in order starting with the **least popular**.

_____   _____   _____   _____   _____

Least popular   **Most popular**

8. What is the value of the 8 and the 7 in the number 78?

7 _____   8 _____

9. Complete the number sentences below.

a) $15 + \boxed{} = 20$ b) $\boxed{} + 45 = 100$

10. Write the symbols x, ÷ or = to make the statements below correct.

a) 45 ☐ 9 ☐ 5

b) 90 ☐ 10 ☐ 9

2 marks

11. What is $\frac{3}{4}$ of 20?

☐

1 mark

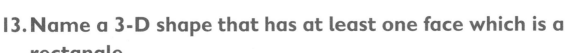 12. Put these lengths in order from longest to shortest.

6 m   50 cm   1.5 m   100 cm   3 m 50 cm

_____ _____ _____ _____ _____

Longest   **Shortest**

5 marks

13. Name a 3-D shape that has at least one face which is a rectangle.

_____

1 mark

14. Fill in the missing numbers on the number line below.

2 marks

15. Complete the number sentences below.

a) 9 + 3 + 7 = ☐

b) 8 + 5 + 2 = ☐

2 marks

PS **16.** Florence says,

"When you multiply 2 numbers together, it doesn't matter what order you do it in. You get the same answer both ways. But when you divide 2 numbers, you must start with the biggest number."

Is Florence correct? Tick the correct answer.

Yes ☐   No ☐

1 mark

PS **17.** At the shop, James needs to pay 45p for a packet of stickers. Write three coins that he could use to make exactly 45p.

_____

1 mark

18. Tick the shapes that have at least one line of symmetry.

1 mark

19. Tick the statements that are correct.

7 − 2 = 2 − 7 ☐

18 − 5 = 5 − 18 ☐

8 + 26 = 26 + 8 ☐

19 + 3 = 3 + 19 ☐

2 marks

PS **20.** A florist plants 36 flowers in small trays. Each tray has 3 flowers.

How many trays does he use? ☐

1 mark

21. Here is a pattern of shapes. Draw the next shape in the pattern.

22. Use this sum to help you fill in the missing numbers below:

28 + 32 = 60

a) ⬚ − 32 = 28

b) 60 − 28 = ⬚

PS 23. Order these periods of time from the shortest to the longest.

2 weeks   13 days   12 months   60 days $\frac{1}{2}$ a year

_____   _____   _____   _____   _____

Shortest   **Longest**

24. Look at the diagram.

North

West   **East**

South

Stuart was facing **south (S)**.

He wants to be facing **west (W)**.

Complete the sentence to describe the **turn** that Stuart needs to make.

Turn ⬚ right-angle in a _____ direction.

25. Write <, > or = to make the number sentences correct.

a) 38 ⬜ 30 + 8

b) 50 + 1 ⬜ 58

c) 91 ⬜ 93 − 3

3 marks

26. Laura has two 50p coins. She spends 90p in the shop. How much change does she get back?

⬜ p

1 mark

27. a) Write the time shown on the clock.

_____

b) Draw hands on the clock to show the time as twenty past 4.

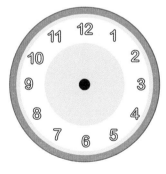

2 marks

Total: ⬜ /60 marks

Answers

English

Page 5
Challenge 1
1. giant, gent, gem circled.

Challenge 2
1. c making a k sound: cat, cliff, cold, claw
   c making a s sound: city, race, rice, fancy

Challenge 3
1.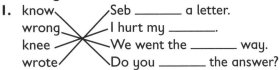
   know   Seb _____ a letter.
   wrong   I hurt my _____.
   knee   We went the _____ way.
   wrote   Do you _____ the answer?

Page 7
Challenge 1
1. squirrel = 2, quantity = 3, middle = 2
   written = 2, energy = 3

Challenge 2
1. Another word for a creature — giraffe
   A very, very big person — hospital
   An animal with a long neck — bottle
   Something a drink might be in — animal
   You might go here if you are ill. — giant

Challenge 3
1. animal, rabbit, wrapping, itself, carefully, blanket, table, middle, pencil, metal, water, bottle, capital, letter, written

Page 9
Challenge 1
1. copy – copied – copier
   reply – replied – replying
   carry – carrying – carried
   fly – flies – flying

Challenge 2
1. a) grump   b) care   c) change   d) enjoy

Challenge 3
1. babies, crying, careful, happier, playful/playing

Page 11
Challenge 1
1. shud — sugar
   shugar — should
   shure — sure

Challenge 2
1. a) could (or should)   b) would   c) should

Challenge 3
1. a) Each word should be read correctly.
   b) Each word should be written correctly
      (1 mark for each).

Page 13
Challenge 1
1. *Goldilocks and the Three Bears* – Who's been eating my… Who's been sitting on my…
   Jack and the Beanstalk – Fee-fi-fo-fum, I smell the blood of…
   Little Red Riding Hood – What big eyes… What big ears…

Challenge 2
1. Examples:
   A giant: a bad person/creature or mythical creature.
   Beans which grow into a beanstalk: magic.
   Cinderella: a poor person or a good person.

Challenge 3
1. a) old
   b) A response that recognises that old is repeated to emphasise the age/history of the castle.

Page 15
Challenge 1
1. 3, 2, 1, 4

Challenge 2
1. a) variety   b) amazed   c) sea

Challenge 3
1. Examples: a) lay   b) climbed   c) quickly

Page 17
Challenge 1
1. Examples: hat; red

Challenge 2
1. a) Milly Mouse
   b) there
   c) sleeps

Challenge 3
1. a) an elephant   b) long, grey
   c) the water is cool/it knows how clever it has been/it likes spraying water on itself

Page 19
Challenge 1
1. a) checks the big cats and feeds them
   b) help them
   c) Their mother was ill.

Challenge 2

1. 'Big cats is the name given to the lions, tigers, leopards and cheetahs.' Because it is a fact about big cats.

Challenge 3

1. It means it is her job to look after them.

Page 21
Challenge 1

1. smiling, grinning – happy
   blubbing, tearful – sad
   shaking, trembling – nervous

Challenge 2

1. She is brave. ✓

Challenge 3

1. a) Nervous. Her hand was shaking./She held her breath./Her tongue was sticking out.
   b) She will win the competition (or a reasonable answer explaining otherwise).

Pages 22–25
Progress test 1: English

1. a) could b) would c) should
2. fly, copy, baby, reply, cry
3. 2, 4, 3, 1
4. a) looked b) tired c) angry
5. icy, nice, city, cell, racing
6. a) training, coaching b) many/lots of
   c) dangerous
7. g as a j sound: magic, age, giant, change, huge
   g as a g sound: gold, log, game
8. a) She was tired. b) stand up quickly c) sulkily
9. a) heavily b) sun c) ice, frost, snow
   d) it is cold/winter, or things don't grow in winter
10. a) 3 b) 2 c) 1 d) 4

Maths
Page 27
Challenge 1

1. 12, 20   15, 24

Challenge 2

1. a) 18, 16, 14   b) 24, 21, 18
   c) 40, 35, 30   d) 61, 51, 41
2. a) 10, 12, 14   b) 21, 24, 27
   c) 40, 45, 50   d) 64, 74, 84

Challenge 3

1. a) 22 b) 15 c) 55 d) 11

Page 29
Challenge 1

1. 2, 7, 13

Challenge 2

1. a) 3 b) 4 c) 6
2. a) 1 b) 2 c) 4

Challenge 3

1. 75, 91, 33
2. 4, 9, 5

Page 31
Challenge 1

1. a) less than   b) more than   c) equal to

Challenge 2

1. Various answers. Examples:
   a) 9 is less than 10
   b) 7 is more than 2
   c) 1 is less than 8
   d) 6 is more than 5
2. 1, 4, 7, 18, 28

Challenge 3

1. a) = b) < c) > d) <

Page 33
Challenge 1

1. 11, eleven
   16, sixteen

Challenge 2

1. 25, twenty-eight, 31, thirty-nine, 41
   72, eighty, 89, ninety-one, 100

Challenge 3

1. a) 9 b) 33 c) 85

Page 35
Challenge 1

1. a) 19, 20, 18, 17
   b) 1, 10, 8, 3
2. a) 10, 19, 2, 5,
   b) 7, 3, 6, 16

Challenge 2

1. 70, 55, 38, 13
2. a) 10   b) 65

Challenge 3

1. a) +, −
   b) +, −
   c) +, +

Page 37
Challenge 1
1. 87
2. 37

Challenge 2
1. 46, 98
2. 34, 51

Challenge 3
1. 55, 81
2. 58, 84

Page 39
Challenge 1
a) $3 + 4 + 7 = 14$ $7 + 3 + 4 = 14$
(or any other combination)
b) $5 + 7 + 5 = 17$ $5 + 5 + 7 = 17$
(or any other combination)

Challenge 3
1.

Repeated addition	Multiplication sentence 1	Multiplication sentence 2
$2 + 2 + 2 = 6$	$3 \times 2 = 6$	$2 \times 3 = 6$
$3 + 3 + 3 + 3 + 3$	$3 \times 5 = 15$	$5 \times 3 = 15$
$2 + 2 = 4$	$2 \times 2 = 4$	$2 \times 2 = 4$
$2 + 2 + 2 + 2 = 8$	$2 \times 4 = 8$	$4 \times 2 = 8$
$5 + 5 + 5 + 5 + 5 = 25$	$5 \times 5 = 25$	$5 \times 5 = 25$
$9 + 9 + 9 + 9 + 9 + 9 + 9$ $+ 9 + 9 + 9 = 90$	$9 \times 10 = 90$	$10 \times 9 = 90$

Page 43
Challenge 1
1. a) 6, 6   b) 4, 4, 4, 4, 4

2. a)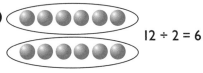
$12 \div 2 = 6$

b)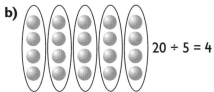
$20 \div 5 = 4$

Challenge 2
1. 10, 4, 2

Challenge 3
1. a) $40 \div 8 = 5$ $40 \div 5 = 8$
b) $22 \div 11 = 2$ $22 \div 2 = 11$
c) $90 \div 10 = 9$ $90 \div 9 = 10$

Challenge 2
1. 4, 6, 2 circled
2. 7, 7, 4 circled
3. 4, 8, 9 (or 5, 7, 9) circled

Challenge 3
1. 15
2. $6 + 9 + 4 = 19$ $4 + 9 + 6 = 19$ $9 + 6 + 4 = 19$
(or any other combination)

Page 41
Challenge 1
1. $2 \times 2 = 4$ $3 \times 2 = 6$ (or $2 \times 3 = 6$)
2. $7 \times 5 = 35$ $5 \times 7 = 35$

Challenge 2
1. a) 16, 18, 20   b) 45, 50, 55   c) 100, 110, 120

Page 45
Challenge 1
1.
$2 \times 6 = 12$

$2 \times 8 = 16$

2.
$12 \div 2 = 6$

Challenge 2
1. a) 28   b) 26
2. a) 8   b) 9

Challenge 3
1. a) $2 \times 11 = 22$
b) $2 \times 24 = 48$
2. a) 18   b) 26

Pages 46–49
Progress test 2: maths
1. **a)** 8, 6, 4   **b)** 6, 3, 0   **c)** 30, 25, 20   **d)** 43, 33, 23
2. 8, 15, 31, 68, 90
3. 6 x 5 = 30   5 x 6 = 30
4. Three from: 26, 29, 69, 62, 96, 92
5. 10, 7, 2
6. 35, 82, 51
7. 70 and 30
8. **a)** 6, 8, 10   **b)** 30, 33, 36   **c)** 50, 55, 60   **d)** 77, 87, 97
9. 5
10. **a)** 20   **b)** 2 x 20 = 40   or 20 x 2 = 40
    c) 20 ÷ 2 = 10
11. 30, 37
12. **a)** 70   **b)** sixty-four
13. £98
14. Three from: 8 + 7 + 9 = 24, 7 + 8 + 9 = 24,
    9 + 8 + 7 = 24, 8 + 9 + 7 = 24, 7 + 9 + 8 = 24,
    9 + 7 + 8 = 24
15. 56 + 38 = 94   94 − 56 = 38   94 − 38 = 56
16. **a)** 24, 50, 70
    b) 5, 11, 9
17. 6 x 2 = 12   2 x 6 = 12
18. 45
19. **a)** >   **b)** =   **c)** <
20. 35
21. 10
22. 18

English
Page 51
Challenge 1
1. Letters traced over accurately. (1 mark for each.)

Challenge 2
1. Letters copied accurately. (1 mark for each.)

Challenge 3
1. Words copied accurately.

Page 53
Challenge 1
1. sh-oo-t, wr-a-pp-i-ng, c-a-tt-le, kn-o-ck

Challenge 2
1. **a)** knight   **b)** two   **c)** meet   **d)** Their   **e)** deer

Challenge 3
1. **a)** The **au** and **se** letters are unusual.
   b) The 'yoo' sound made be **eau** is unusual.

2. Examples: **a)** bluebell, blueberry   **b)** backbone,
   backlog   **c)** rainbow, rainforest   **d)** teapot,
   teaspoon

Page 55
Challenge 1
1. **a)** couldn't   **b)** I'll   **c)** She's   **d)** can't

Challenge 2
1. **a)** mum's   **b)** dog's (or dogs')   **c)** Zak's   **d)** Noah's

Challenge 3
1. can't, friend's (or friends'), It's, We're, Daisy's

Page 57
Challenge 1
1. run, nice, hope, happy, pat, thought

Challenge 2
1. The explanation should show an understanding
   that the **e** is dropped from the root word before
   adding the endings **-er/-ing**.

Challenge 3
1. **a) run/runner** – the explanation should show an
      understanding that the consonant at the end of
      the word is doubled before adding the suffix.
   b) happy/happily – the explanation should show
      an understanding that the y at the end of the
      word becomes 'i' before adding the suffix.

Page 59
Challenge 1
1. 1 mark for a clear explanation of the beginning,
   middle and end of the chosen story, and 1 mark for
   identification of main character(s) and setting(s).

Challenge 2
1. It was a dark, wet day. – beginning
   Finally, they made it. What a great adventure it
   had been! – end
   The children were brave but they knew their
   problems were not over. – middle

Challenge 3
1. 1 mark for each correctly formed sentence (each
   of which must contain at least one adjective).

Page 61
Challenge 1
1. 1 mark for each idea which must relate to the
   question prompt.

Challenge 2

I. 1 mark for a correctly formed sentence that contains at least one adjective.

Challenge 3

I. 1 mark for each sentence. Examples:
First, put the seed in the soil.
Next, water the seed.
Eventually, your plant will grow.

Page 63
Challenge 1

I. Examples: smelly, rotten, mouldy.

Challenge 2

I. Examples: **a)** We went for a walk to the park, then came home because it was dark **b)** The girl tapped her feet, as she danced along the street.

Challenge 3

I. At least one adjective related to sight, sound, smell, touch or taste. Examples: **a)** delicious, smooth chocolate **b)** loud, banging drum **c)** sweet, scented flower

Page 65
Challenge 1

I. Dear, Thank, party, I, Spain, there

Challenge 2

I. Full stop after party. Question mark after their/there.

Challenge 3

I. A reasonable adjective to replace 'nice' in a coherent sentence: Example: The beach was **beautiful** and the sea was **calm**.

Page 67
Challenge 1

I. **a)** command **b)** exclamation
c) question **d)** statement

Challenge 2

I. **a)** Example: Where was the dog last seen?
b) Example: The dog is called Skip.

Challenge 3

I. 1 mark for each sentence, properly punctuated, which matches the sentence type.

Page 69
Challenge 1

I. **a)** Example: white **b)** Example: tasty
c) Example: huge **d)** Example: tiny

Challenge 2

I. **a)** Example: crazy dog
b) Example: delicious cake
c) Example: amazing view
d) Example: lovely lady

Challenge 3

I. 1 mark for each expanded noun phrase; 1 mark for each correctly punctuated sentence.
a) Example: Amir lives in a fantastic, old house.
b) Example: Henry ate the huge, juicy burger.

Page 71
Challenge 1

I. **a)** and **b)** or **c)** but **d)** and

Challenge 2

I. **a)** The snow melted quickly **because** it was a warm day.
b) The snow will melt **if** the sun keeps shining.
c) The snow is melting **but** at least it is warm now.

Challenge 3

I. **a)** Example: I am hungry but I forgot my sandwiches.
b) Example: You will get told off if you are naughty.

Page 73
Challenge 1

I. **a)** were running **b)** was writing **c)** climbed

Challenge 2

I. **a)** sailing **b)** skipping **c)** talking

Challenge 3

a) Example: Yesterday, I was sleeping in my bedroom.
b) Example: Today, we are playing in the garden.
c) Example: Yesterday, they were baking delicious cakes.

Pages 74–77
Progress test 3: English

1. **a)** There **b)** brakes **c)** to **d)** knew
2. **a)** or **b)** but **c)** because **d)** if
3. **a)** Finn's **b)** Grandma's **c)** cat's (or cats')
   d) Stan's
4. **a)** 1 **b)** 3 **c)** 2 **d)** 3 **e)** 3 **f)** 4

5. a) two years **b)** helps **c)** records
  d) The answer should refer to the fact that Stephi is a schoolgirl doing some park ranger jobs.
  e) A reasonable choice of word to replace 'likes', in a coherent sentence. Example: She **loves** the outdoors and wildlife, and she **enjoys** helping.
6. a) ! exclamation **b)** ? question
  c) . command **d)** . statement
7. a) there **b)** see **c)** hear **d)** night **e)** bare
  f) blue
8. A reasonable description containing at least two adjectives. Examples: Colourful, bright flowers; Crisp, white snow; A shiny, new car.
9. a) Example: Dad chased the fluffy pet rabbit.
  b) Example: Grace lost her new school bag.
10. a) the bell **b)** the children
  c) happy/happily **d)** it's

Maths

Page 79
Challenge 1

1. ✓

2.  ✓

Challenge 2

1. ✓

2. ✓

Challenge 3
1. 2 + 2 + 2 + 2 circled
2. 1 + 1 + 1 circled
3. 10 + 10 circled

Page 81
Challenge 1

1. Examples: **a)**  **b)**

2. Examples: **a)**  **b)**

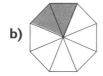

Challenge 2
1. 3 spots circled. $12 \div 4 = 3$
2. 5 spots circled. $15 \div 3 = 5$
3. 12 spots circled. $16 \div 4 = 4$ $4 \times 3 = 12$

Challenge 3
1.

Number	$\frac{1}{2}$	$\frac{1}{4}$	$\frac{1}{3}$	$\frac{3}{4}$
8	4	2		6
12	6	3	4	9
16	8	4		12
18	9		6	
24	12	6	8	18

Page 83
Challenge 1
1. D, A, C, B, E
2. Accept 9, 10, 11, 12 or 13 cm

Challenge 2
1. a) <   **b)** <   **c)** =

Challenge 3
1. a) 3 litres   **b)** 3,000 ml

Page 85
Challenge 1
1. a) 10p   **b)** £4 and 50p

Challenge 2
1. In any order:

Combination 1	50p + 20p + 10p
Combination 2	50p + 20p + 5p + 5p
Combination 3	50p + 10p + 10p + 5p + 5p

2.

Pounds	Pence	Total
4	35	£ 4 and 35 p
6	74	£ 6 and 74 p
9	41	£ 9 and 41 p

Challenge 3
1. £10, £10, £10
2. £15 and 60p

Page 87
Challenge 1
1. a) 1 o'clock   **b)** quarter past 9

Challenge 2

1. a)
   b)
   c)
   d)

Challenge 3

1. a) 2 o'clock
   b) twenty to 4

Page 89
Challenge 1

1. ✓   ✓

Challenge 2

1. Oval: 1, 0
   Semi-circle: 2, 2
   Triangle: 3, 3
   Rectangle: 4, 4

Challenge 3

1.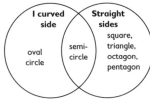

I curved side: oval, circle

semi-circle

Straight sides: square, triangle, octagon, pentagon

Page 91
Challenge 1

1.

Shape	Name	Faces	Edges	Vertices
	Cone	2	1	1
	Cylinder	3	2	0
	Pyramid	4	6	4

Challenge 2

1. cylinder

Challenge 3

1. a) Rectangle, triangle
   b) Square, rectangle
   c) Square, triangle

Page 93
Challenge 1

1. a) circle   b) oval   c) rectangle
   d) rectangle   e) hexagon

2.

Challenge 2

1. Answers will vary. The repeating pattern must have no more than four shapes and include a circle, a square and a triangle.

Challenge 3

1.

2. Example: The next three shapes will be a red square, a red square and a blue triangle.

Page 95
Challenge 1

1. a) Crocodile   b) 2   c) 6

Challenge 2

1. a) crocodile   b) crab   c) palm tree

Challenge 3

1. Turtle correctly drawn on island as shown:

Page 97
Challenge 1
1.

Favourite fruit	Tally
Apple	JHT I
Banana	III
Pear	II
Orange	JHT IIII
Strawberry	JHT II

Challenge 2
1.

Apple	♀♀♀♀♀♀
Banana	♀♀♀
Pear	♀♀
Orange	♀♀♀♀♀♀♀♀♀
Strawberry	♀♀♀♀♀♀♀

Challenge 3
1. **a)** orange
   b) pear
   c) 3
   d) 2
   e) 27

Page 99
Challenge 1
1.

Favourite colour	Tally
Red	JHT JHT JHT
Green	JHT JHT
Blue	JHT JHT JHT JHT
Yellow	JHT
Purple	JHT JHT JHT JHT JHT
Pink	JHT JHT

Challenge 2
1.

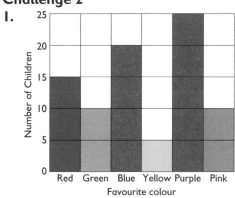

Challenge 3
1. **a)** purple   **b)** 25   **c)** yellow
   d) 10   **e)** 85

Pages 100–103
Progress test 4: maths
1. Example:

2. 6 marbles circled

3.

4. >, =, <
5. **a)**    **b)**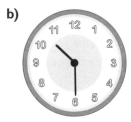

6. **a)**

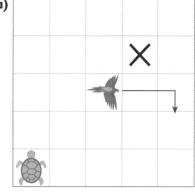

   b) 2, quarter, clockwise
7. Sphere, 1, 0, 0
8. 4, 4, 10, 21
9. 1 metre and 20 cm or 120 cm
10. **a)** half past 9   **b)** quarter past 11
11. $\frac{1}{2}$ or $\frac{2}{4}$ or $\frac{4}{8}$
12. Triangular prism ✓
13. **a)**   **b)**

14. (shapes)

15. a)

Vehicle	Tally	Total
Car	ⅢⅠⅢⅠ	10
Lorry	ⅢⅠ ⅠⅠⅠⅠ	9
Bus	ⅢⅠ ⅠⅠⅠ	8
Motorbike	ⅠⅠⅠⅠ	4
Van	ⅠⅠⅠ	3
Bicycle	Ⅰ	1

b) car   **c)** 6

d) Lorry and Bicycle

e) Answers may vary. Example: Which type of vehicle drove past the least?

16. Pentagon, 5, 5

17. Example:

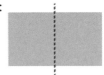

Pages 104–109
English mixed questions

1. **a)** knocked **b)** written **c)** know **d)** gnaw
2. **a)** practise **b)** making costumes, changing scenery
    c) Accept a reasonable answer that suggests, for example, he might not want to do it in front of an audience or that he is afraid of making a mistake.
3. **a)** You're **b)** couldn't **c)** I'll **d)** aren't **e)** She's
4. replied, tried, carried, copying, flying
5. **a)** is running **b)** is eating
    c) are pouring **d)** are drawing
6. **a)** hike **b)** shine **c)** baby **d)** care
    e) happy **f)** plenty
7. **a)** You will be dizzy **if** you keep spinning round.
    b) We are going home now **because** it is getting dark.
    c) The car was old **but** at least it still worked.
8. **a)** Examples: enjoyed, loved
    b) Examples: filthy, untidy
    c) Examples: yelled, shrieked
9. Three correctly formed sentences, each of which must contain at least one adjective.
10. A correctly formed sentence which matches each sentence type.
11. **a)** Example: First, put toothpaste on the toothbrush.
    b) Example: Next, brush your teeth.
12. **a)** She is determined. ✓
    b) Example: She enters a race and wins.
13. **a)** Example: big dog **b)** Example: empty plate
    c) Example: frozen ground **d)** Example: old shop
14. 2 marks for any reasonable adverbs. Examples:
    a) The tortoise walked slowly along the road.
    b) The hare ran far ahead of the tortoise.

15. a) mum's **b)** Tom's **c)** boy's (or boys')
    d) friend's

16. a) sea **b)** smooth grey humps **c)** jump
    d) bright, white

Pages 110–118
Maths mixed questions

1. 3, 12
2. 5
3. **a)** 10 **b)** 18
4. **a)** $\frac{3}{4}$ **b)** $\frac{6}{8}$ or $\frac{3}{4}$
5. Length of a car – metres
    Mass of a person – kilograms
    Capacity of a bath – litres
    Length of a pen – centimetres
6. 8 edges, 5 faces, 5 vertices
7. **a)** ⅢⅠ Ⅰ
    b) Scooter
    c) Skateboard, Roller skates, Tricycle, Scooter, Bike
8. 7 tens, 8 ones
9. **a)** 5 **b)** 55
10. **a)** =, x OR ÷, =   **b)** ÷, = OR =, ×
11. 15
12. 6 m, 3 m 50 cm, 1.5 m, 100 cm, 50 cm
13. Cuboid or triangular prism
14. 40, 80
15. **a)** 19 **b)** 15
16. Yes ✓
17. 20p + 20p + 5p
18.
 ✓, ✓, ✓, ✓

19. 8 + 26 = 26 + 8 ✓
    19 + 3 = 3 + 19 ✓

20. 12
21.

22. **a)** 60 **b)** 32
23. 13 days, 2 weeks, 60 days, $\frac{1}{2}$ a year, 12 months
24. 1, clockwise
25. **a)** = **b)** < **c)** >
26. 10p
27. **a)** Quarter past 8
    b)

English glossary

Adjective   A word used to describe things such as colour, size or other features of an object or person (noun).

Adverb   A word used to give more information about a verb, such as to describe the way something is done, e.g. quietly, slowly, quickly, carefully.

Apostrophe   'A punctuation mark used to:
- replace missing letters in contracted words, e.g. I am – I'm, we will – we'll
- show belonging, e.g. Dad's hat, the car's wheels.

Clause   A group of words which includes a subject and a verb.

Comma   , A punctuation mark used to separate items in a list and show different parts of a sentence.

Command   A sentence type which gives an order, and includes a verb, e.g. Come here, now.

Common exception word   A word that does not follow a spelling rule or cannot be easily sounded out when segmented.

Composition   Putting together a piece of writing.

Compound word   Words made up from two or more words, e.g. play + ground = playground

Contraction   A word made from shortening two words and replacing the missing letter(s) with an apostrophe.

Cursive   Formation of letters which allows them to be joined together when writing.

Editing   Making changes to writing to improve it.

Exclamation   A sentence type in which something is being stressed or highlighted, e.g. What a fantastic day it has been!

Expanded noun phrase   A phrase containing two or more words with a noun as its head, e.g. the huge farm, a raging storm, some naughty children.

Fiction   A made-up story.

Glossary   An alphabetical list in a non-fiction book, giving key words and their meanings.

Graphemes   The letter or letters which represent a sound in a word, e.g. c-a-t or sh-o-p.

Homophone   A word that sounds the same or nearly the same as another word but has a different meaning.

Inference   Using clues in a text to decide how or why something has happened, or how and why a character acts or feels a certain way.

Joining word   A word used to join two words, phrases or clauses, e.g. and, or, but. The words because, that and when can be used to join two clauses.

Non-fiction   Writing about facts, e.g. information texts, recounts or instructions.

Noun   A naming word for a person, place or thing.

Past tense   Used to indicate that something happened (in the past).

Present tense   Used to indicate that something is happening now (in the present).

Phonemes   Sounds made in speech, usually corresponding to a letter or group of letters.

Plan   A plan for a piece of writing which shows what the main points will be and the parts it will be organised into.

Plural   More than one.

Poem   A type of writing that describes something or tells a story, often using rhyming words or repeating words.

Possession   The use of the apostrophe to show belonging, e.g. the man's car.

Prediction   Working out what may happen next in a text or a story, usually by thinking about what has already happened and using clues from that.

Pronoun   A word that replaces a noun or noun phrase, e.g. he, she, they.

Proofreading   Reading through writing to check for sense and mistakes.

Question   A sentence used to ask something. Questions often start with the words: What, Where, When, Who, How or Why. They end with a question mark.

Recurring language   A sentence or group of words which is repeated a number of times in a story or poem.

Rhyme   Two or more words where the final sound is the same, e.g. fish, dish.

Root word   A word before any further letters are added which alter the meaning, e.g. jump which can become jumper, jumped or jumping.

Segmenting   Separating words into smaller chunks.

Sequence   A group of sentences or ideas that are spoken or written in order.

Silent letters   Letters that are used in the spelling of words but cannot be heard when the word is spoken, e.g. the 'k' in knee and the first 'k' in knock.

Singular   Only one.

Statement   A sentence that gives information.

Suffix   A letter or letters added to the end of a root word which changes the word meaning.

Syllable   A 'beat' in a word. Each syllable contains a vowel sound.

Theme   A central idea of a story, e.g. magic, friendship.

Verb   A 'doing', 'being' or 'having' word, e.g. She **reads** her book, I **am** tired, Zak **has** a new pen.

Vowel   The letters a, e, i, o and u.

Maths glossary

Addition   Finding the total value of two or more numbers. Shown by the symbol **+**.

Analogue clock   A clock that shows the time using an hour hand to indicate the hour and a minute hand to indicate minutes.

Anti-clockwise   A direction of a turn to the left, the opposite way to the hands of a clock.

Array   A pictorial representation of multiplication and division. Typically shown as rows of dots.

Block graph   A visual way of showing data in the form of blocks or bars.

Capacity   How much a container can hold; can be measured in millilitres (ml) or litres (l).

Circle   A 2-D shape with 1 curved face and no vertices.

Clockwise   A direction of a turn to the right as if following the hands of a clock.

Column number system   Also known as the place value headers; describes the value of a digit as Hundreds, Tens or Ones.

Commutativity   When two numbers are added or multiplied, it can be done in any order and the same answer will be obtained. Addition and multiplication have commutativity (subtraction and division do not).

Cone   A 3-D shape with 2 faces (1 circular), 1 edge and 1 vertex.

Cube   A 3-D shape with 6 square faces, 12 edges and 8 vertices.

Cuboid   A 3-D shape with 6 faces (some or all of which are rectangular), 12 edges and 8 vertices.

Currency   A country's system of money.

Cylinder   A 3-D shape with 2 circular faces, 1 rectangular face, 2 edges and no vertices.

Data   Information.

Denominator   In a fraction, the number below the line. The number of parts in the whole.

Digit   Number or numeral; the way we represent a number or amount.

Division   The process of splitting a number up into equal parts, and finding how many equal parts can be made and whether there is a remainder. It is shown by the symbol ÷.

Estimate   Using logical thinking to have a good guess at something in maths, using facts you already know.

Even numbers   Numbers that always end in 0, 2, 4, 6 or 8.

Face   Any surface of a 3-D shape. Faces can be flat or curved, and many different shapes.

Factor   One of two or more numbers that divides a given number without a remainder. In the number sentence 6 x 3 = 18, both 6 and 3 are factors of 18.

Fraction   A number that represents part of a whole, e.g. $\frac{1}{2}$.

Half   When something has been split into two equal parts or numbers.

Hexagon   A 2-D shape with 6 sides and 6 corners.

Inverse   The calculation which is opposite to a given calculation, and effectively reverses it. Addition is the inverse of subtraction; multiplication is the inverse of division.

Length (height)   How long something is; measured in centimetres (cm), metres (m) or kilometres (km).

Mass/weight   How heavy something is; measured in grams (g) or kilograms (kg).

Multiplication   Finding how many altogether in a given number of equal sized groups. Represented by the symbol **x**.

Number bonds   Pairs of numbers that add up to a specific number.

Number facts   Basic addition, subtraction, multiplication and division calculations. Examples include number bonds and multiplication tables.

Number line   A visual representation of numbers along a horizontal line.

Numerator   In a fraction, the number above the line.

Odd numbers   All whole numbers which are not exactly divisible by 2. Odd numbers always end in 1, 3, 5, 7 or 9.

Octagon   A 2-D shape with 8 sides and 8 corners.

Operation   The four mathematical operations are addition, subtraction, multiplication and division.

Ordering   Putting numbers in the correct order according to size, e.g. smallest to largest (ascending order) or largest to smallest (descending order). Also involves using greater than, less than and equals symbols (<, > and =).

Partitioning   Splitting a number down into smaller more manageable parts, e.g. 23 can be split into 20 and 3.

Pictogram   A way of showing data visually using pictures and a key to show what the data is worth, to allow a comparison of results collected.

Place value   The value of a digit; where it is placed within the number.

Pentagon   A 2-D shape with 5 sides and 5 corners.

Position   Where an object is. For example, the cup is on the table. Position can be where an object is in comparison to another object.

Prism   A 3-D shape with flat sides and identically shaped end faces. The cross section of a prism is the same all the way through. Examples are a triangular prism and a hexagonal prism.

Product   The result of multiplying two numbers together.

Pyramid   A 3-D shape with 4 triangular faces and 4 vertices.

Recombining   Putting a number back together. This is the opposite of partitioning.

Rectangle   A 2-D shape with 4 straight sides and 4 right angles. Opposite sides are the same length.

Repeated addition   A way of teaching about multiplication as the repeated grouping of the same number, e.g. 4 x 2 is the same as 2 + 2 + 2 + 2.

Repeated subtraction   Using subtraction for division as the repeated subtraction of the same number down to zero, e.g. 15 ÷ 3 using repeated subtraction would be: 15 − 3 − 3 − 3 − 3 − 3 = 0.

Sequence   A set pattern of numbers or shapes.

Sphere   A 3-D shape with 1 curved face, no edges and no vertices.

Square   A 2-D shape with 4 equal sides, 4 corners and 4 right angles.

Square-based pyramid   A 3-D shape with 4 triangular faces, 1 square face and 5 vertices.

Subtraction   Taking one number away from another; finding the difference between two numbers. Shown by the symbol −.

Symmetry   When a shape can be split in half equally, e.g. a square has four lines of symmetry. This mean it can be split in half in four different ways.

Tally chart   A way of recording information in groups of 5; shown by four lines with a line through.

Triangle   A 2-D shape with 3 straight sides and 3 corners; (can be equilateral, isosceles, right-angled or scalene).

Turn   A movement in a space, either clockwise or anti-clockwise. (A quarter turn is 90°, a half turn is 180°, a three-quarter turn is 270° and a full turn is 360°.)

Unit fraction   A fraction where the numerator is 1 and the denominator is a whole number.

Vertex/vertices   The place on a 3-D shape where edges meet.

Whole number   A number that contains no fractions, e.g. 1 and a $\frac{1}{2}$ is not a whole number.

2-D shapes   Shapes that are flat and have two dimensions – height/length and width.

3-D shapes   Shapes that have a solid form and have three dimensions – height/length, width and depth.

Acknowledgements

The authors and publisher are grateful to the copyright holders for permission to use quoted materials and images.
All images are ©Shutterstock.com and ©HarperCollins*Publishers*
Every effort has been made to trace copyright holders and obtain their permission for the use of copyright material. The authors and publisher will gladly receive information enabling them to rectify any error or omission in subsequent editions. All facts are correct at time of going to press.
Published by Collins
An imprint of HarperCollins*Publishers*
1 London Bridge Street
London SE1 9GF

HarperCollins*Publishers*
Macken House, 39/40 Mayor Street Upper,
Dublin 1, D01 C9W8, Ireland
ISBN: 978-0-00-839878-1
First published 2020
10 9 8

British Library Cataloguing in Publication Data.
A CIP record of this book is available from the British Library.
Authors: Jon Goulding and Brad Thompson
Publisher: Fiona McGlade
Project Development: Katie Galloway
Cover Design: Kevin Robbins and Sarah Duxbury
Inside Concept Design: Ian Wrigley
Page Layout: Q2A Media
Production: Karen Nulty
Printed in India by Multivista Global Pvt. Ltd.

MIX
Paper | Supporting responsible forestry
FSC™ C007454

This book is produced from independently certified FSC™ paper to ensure responsible forest management.

For more information visit: www.harpercollins.co.uk/green

Progress charts

Use these charts to record your results in the four Progress Tests. Colour in the questions that you got right to help you identify any areas that you might need to study and practise again. (These areas are indicated in the 'See page…' row in the charts.)

Progress test 1: English

	Q1	Q2	Q3	Q4	Q5	Q6	Q7	Q8	Q9	Q10	TOTAL /45
See page...	10	8	14	14	4	18	4	20	16	6	

Progress test 2: Maths

	Q1	Q2	Q3	Q4	Q5	Q6	Q7	Q8	Q9	Q10	Q11	TOTAL /48
See page...	26	30	40	28	36	36	34	40	40	44	28	
	Q12	Q13	Q14	Q15	Q16	Q17	Q18	Q19	Q20	Q21	Q22	
See page...	32	36	38	36	40	40	36	30	26	42	44	

Well done

Progress test 3: English

	Q1	Q2	Q3	Q4	Q5	Q6	Q7	Q8	Q9	Q10	TOTAL /46
See page...	52	70	54	6	18, 60	66	52	68	68	16	

Progress test 4: Maths

	Q1	Q2	Q3	Q4	Q5	Q6	Q7	Q8	Q9	Q10	Q11	Q12	Q13	Q14	Q15	Q16	Q17	TOTAL /44
See page...	78	80	82	82	86	94	90	80	82	86	78	90	86	92	96	88	88	

Use this table to record your results for the Mixed questions sections on pages 104 –115.

English mixed questions	Total score:	/ 66 marks
Maths mixed questions	Total score:	/ 60 marks